D1187508

EARTH SCIENCE

EARTH SCIENCE

The People Behind the Science

KATHERINE CULLEN, PH.D.

CHELSEA HOUSE
PUBLISHERS

An imprint of Infobase Publishing

Earth Science: The People Behind the Science

Copyright © 2006 by Katherine Cullen, Ph.D.

Chelsea House
An imprint of Infobase Publishing
132 West 31st Street
New York NY 10001

Library of Congress Cataloging-in-Publication Data

Cullen, Katherine E.
  Earth science: the people behind the science/Katherine Cullen.
    p. cm. — (Pioneers in science)
  Includes bibliographical references and index.
  ISBN 0-8160-5464-9 (hardcover)
  1. Earth scientists Biography. 2. Earth science—History. I. Title. II. Series.
  QE21.C85 2005
  550'.92'2—dc22   2005022171

Chelsea House books are available at special discounts when purchased in bulk quantities for businesses, associations, institutions, or sales promotions. Please call our Special Sales Department in New York at (212) 967-8800 or (800) 322-8755.

You can find Chelsea House on the World Wide Web at
http://www.chelseahouse.com

Text design by Mary Susan Ryan-Flynn
Cover design by Cathy Rincon
Illustrations by Bobbi McCutcheon

Printed in the United States of America

MP FOF 10 9 8 7 6 5 4 3 2

This book is printed on acid-free paper.

*I dedicate this book to
all future pioneers in science.*

☙

CONTENTS

Preface   xiii

Acknowledgments   xvii

Introduction   xix

CHAPTER 1
Georgius Agricola (1494–1555): The Forefather of Geology and the Father of Mineralogy   1

"Peasant Farmer"   2
An Expert on Mining   3
Mining and Metallurgy   4
A Prolific Author   4
On Metallurgy   6
Chronology   9
Further Reading   10

CHAPTER 2
Nicolaus Steno (1638–1686): The Law of Superposition of Rock Layers and the Principles of Original Horizontality and Lateral Extension   13

An Interest in Science   14
The Seashell Question   15
Discovery of a Salivary Duct   16
Questioning Descartes   17
Cartesian Philosophy   18

Studies on Muscular Contraction   20
Glossopetrae   21
A Forerunner   24
Devotion to Catholic Missions   26
Chronology   28
Further Reading   29

CHAPTER 3

James Hutton (1726–1797): Uniformitarianism as the
  Central Principle of Historical Geology   31

A Lawyer's Apprentice   32
Geological and Agricultural Studies   32
"Theory of the Earth"   33
The Effect of Natural Processes on the
    Shape of the Earth   35
Opposition   38
Support for Hutton's Theory   40
Chronology   40
Further Reading   42

CHAPTER 4

Alexander von Humboldt (1769–1859): Unification of the
  Natural Sciences   43

A Career in Politics or Mining   44
An Exotic Expedition   45
Volcanoes   48
Highest Altitude   50
The Larger Task That Lay Ahead   53
Diamonds in the Urals   55
Geomagnetism   57
Cosmic Comprehension   58
Chronology   59
Further Reading   60

CHAPTER 5

Georges Cuvier (1769–1832): The Reality of Extinction of Past Life-forms — 61

Birth in Montbéliard	62
A Man with Many Titles	62
Identification of Animals from Fossil Remains	64
Fossils and Paleontology	*64*
Extinction and Catastrophism	67
Still an Anatomist	71
Cuvier's Legacy	72
Chronology	73
Further Reading	74

CHAPTER 6

William Smith (1769–1839): Creation of the World's First Geological Map — 77

Pound Stones	78
Career as a Surveyor	78
The Birth of Stratigraphy	82
Mary Anning	*84*
The World's First Geological Map	87
Respected at Last	90
Chronology	91
Further Reading	92

CHAPTER 7

Sir Charles Lyell (1797–1875): The Gradual Nature of Earth's Processes — 93

Preference of Geology over Law	94
Uniformity Revealed	95
William Buckland	*96*
Principles and Elements	99
Expertise Abroad	100

The Age of Man   101
Knighthood and Baronetcy   102
Chronology   103
Further Reading   104

CHAPTER 8

Alfred Wegener (1880–1930): The Theory of Continental Drift   105

From Astronomy to Meteorology   106
A Land-Moving Theory   107
A Revolution from International Controversy   111
Plate Tectonics   *112*
A Bitter Cold Ending   114
Chronology   115
Further Reading   116

CHAPTER 9

Arthur Holmes (1890–1965): Estimation of the Earth's Age   117

The 20-Million-Year Dispute   118
Entrance to the Dating Game   120
Mozambique   122
Carbon Dating   *122*
The Problem with Lead   124
Misfortune and Providence   125
The Powerful Engine of Radioactivity   126
A Fourth Isotope   127
Primeval Lead Composition   128
The End of Time for a Famous Geologist   132
Chronology   133
Further Reading   134

CHAPTER 10

Stephen Jay Gould (1941–2002): Theory of Punctuated Equilibrium   137

A Young Boy's Interest in Paleontology   138
Evolution by Jerks   139

Darwin's View   *140*

A Prolific and Influential Writer   143

A New Structure for Evolutionary Theory   144

Reflections and Miscellany   147

Chronology   148

Further Reading   149

Glossary   151

Further Resources   159

Index   167

PREFACE

Being first in line earns a devoted fan the best seat in the stadium. The first runner to break the ribbon spanning the finish line receives a gold medal. The firstborn child inherits the royal throne. Certain advantages or privileges often accompany being the first, but sometimes the price paid is considerable. Neil Armstrong, the first man to walk on the Moon, began flying lessons at age 16, toiled at numerous jobs to pay tuition, studied diligently to earn his bachelor's degree in aerospace engineering, flew 78 combat missions in Korea as a brave navy pilot, worked as a civilian test pilot for seven years, then as an astronaut for NASA for another seven years, and made several dangerous trips into space before the historic *Apollo 11* mission. He endured rigorous physical and mental preparation, underwent years of training, and risked his life to courageously step foot where no man had ever walked before. Armstrong was a pioneer of space exploration; he opened up the way for others to follow. Not all pioneering activities may be as perilous as space exploration. But like the ardent fan, a pioneer in science must be dedicated; like the competitive runner, she must be committed; and like being born to royalty, sometimes providence plays a role.

Science encompasses all knowledge based on general truths or observed facts. More narrowly defined, science refers to a branch of knowledge that specifically deals with the natural world and its laws. Philosophically described, science is an endeavor, a search for truth, a way of knowing, or a means of discovering. Scientists gain information through employing a procedure called the scientific method. The scientific method requires one to state the problem and formulate a testable hypothesis or educated guess to describe a phenomenon or explain an observation, test the hypothesis experimentally or by collecting data from observations, and draw conclusions from the results. Data can eliminate a hypothesis, but never confirm it with absolute certainty; scientists may accept a hypothesis as true when sufficient supporting evidence has been obtained. The process sounds entirely straightforward, but sometimes advancements in science do not follow such a logical approach. Because humans make the observations, generate the hypothesis, carry out the experiments, and draw the conclusions, students of science must recognize the personal dimension of science.

Pioneers in Science is a set of volumes that profile the people behind the science, individuals who initiated new lines of thought or research. They risked possible failure and often faced opposition but persisted to pave new pathways of scientific exploration. Their backgrounds vary tremendously; some never graduated from secondary school, while others earned multiple advanced degrees. Familial affluence allowed some to pursue research unhindered by financial concerns, but others were so poor they suffered from malnutrition or became homeless. Personalities ranged from exuberant to somber and gentle to stubborn, but they all sacrificed, giving their time, insight, and commitment because they believed in the pursuit of knowledge. The desire to understand kept them going when they faced difficulties, and their contributions moved science forward.

The set consists of eight separate volumes: *Biology; Chemistry; Earth Science; Marine Science; Physics; Science, Technology, and Society; Space and Astronomy;* and *Weather and Climate.* Each book contains 10 biographical sketches of pioneering individuals in a subject, including information about their childhood, how they entered into their scientific careers, their research, and enough background science information for the reader to appreciate their discoveries and contributions. Though all the profiled individuals are certainly distinguished, their inclusion is not intended to imply that they are the greatest scientists of all time. Rather, the profiled individuals were selected to reflect a variety of subdisciplines in each field, different histories, alternative approaches to science, and diverse characters.

Each chapter includes a chronology and a list of specific references about the individual and his work. Each book also includes an introduction to the field of science to which its pioneers contributed, line illustrations, photographs, a glossary of scientific terms related to the research described in the text, and a listing of further resources for information about the general subject matter.

The goal of this set is to provide, at an appropriate level, factual information about pioneering scientists. The authors hope that readers will be inspired to achieve greatness themselves, to feel connected to the people behind science, and to believe that they may have a positive and enduring impact on society.

ACKNOWLEDGMENTS

I would like to thank Frank K. Darmstadt, Executive Editor of science and mathematics at Infobase Publishing, for his skillful guidance and extreme patience, and to Melissa Cullen-DuPont, his assistant. Appreciation is also extended to illustrator Bobbi McCutcheon for her dedicated professionalism and to Ann E. Hicks and Amy L. Conver for their constructive suggestions. The reference librarians and support staff of the main branch of the Medina County District Library, located in Medina, Ohio, deserve acknowledgment for their assistance in obtaining interlibrary loans, acquiring numerous special requests, and handling the hundreds of materials and resources the author borrowed during the writing of this set. Gratitude is also expressed to Pam Shirk, former media specialist at A. I. Root Middle School in Medina, Ohio, for sharing her expertise. Many people and organizations generously gave permission to use their photographs. Their names are acknowledged underneath the donated images. Thank you all.

INTRODUCTION

Humans have long pondered the origin and the history of the Earth in search of the meaning and purpose for their existence in this world. Though ancient Greek philosophers first used reason and observation to develop the natural sciences, after the popularization of Christianity, the biblical account of creation and the story of a great deluge dominated beliefs about the Earth's origin and history until the Scientific Revolution and the Age of Enlightenment. The major result of these two European intellectual movements that began in the late 1500s and lasted until the 1800s was the emphasis placed on the importance of observation and experimentation in order to make scientific progress. Naturalists examined the Earth with scrutiny and drew conclusions based on evidence, rather than relying on speculation or supernatural phenomena. Reliance upon observation suggested that strata were laid down naturally, that earthquakes and volcanoes transformed the Earth's structure, and that erosion played a significant role in shaping the Earth's surface. These major discoveries in the field of *geology* greatly advanced the *Earth sciences*. During the 19th century, the belief that the Earth's features resulted from sudden cataclysmic catastrophes, called *catastrophism*, became popular, and some scientists attempted to reconcile a history of floods and earthquakes with events recorded in the Bible and a young age of 6,000 years. *Uniformitarianism*, the belief that the Earth has been shaped continuously over immense periods of geological time by processes that still operate today, replaced catastrophism as the most accepted theory for the formation of the Earth's physical features. Today scientists subscribe to a more balanced view, believing that both gradual processes and catastrophes have played important roles during the Earth's history.

Earth science is the study of the Earth, its origin, its structure, the changes it has undergone, and the past and future consequences of those changes. The field can be divided into four major branches. *Meteorology* is the scientific study of the atmosphere and the variations in conditions such as wind, moisture, temperature, and pressure that affect weather. *Oceanography*, the science of the oceans, encompasses all natural sciences (such as biology, chemistry, geology, and physics) as they are applied to a marine environment. The branch of *astronomy* deals with all matter in the universe and examines the effects of Earth on and by other objects within the cosmos. Geology is the science that deals with the Earth's crust, its composition, and its history. Often scientific research can be classified into more than one discipline. For example, though the study of the composition of the ocean basin is considered an aspect of physical oceanography, it may also be called marine geology. Because pioneering meteorologists, oceanographers, and astronomers are prominently profiled in other books of this set, specifically, *Weather and Climate*, *Marine Science*, and *Space and Astronomy*, the main focus of the scientists profiled in this title, *Earth Science*, is geology.

Geologists study the material components of the Earth's surface and interior, as well as the natural processes that occur on the Earth. They apply information and methods from chemistry, physics, and biology to learn about the components of the planet, land, water, and air. While *physical geologists* are concerned with the material components of the Earth and the processes that act upon them, *historical geologists* focus on the origin of the planet and the changes that have occurred during the past 4.6 billion years. The two complement each other in that historical geologists depend on geochemical and geophysical evidence to draw their conclusions, and naturally, the present structure and composition of Earth materials directly result from the past processes and events.

Though clues to the Earth's origin, structure, and history have always been present, the field of Earth science has evolved, just as the Earth, through the development of new methodologies and interpretations by pioneering scientists such as the ones described in this book. Disciplines such as mining and metallurgy have been recognized as economically important for thousands of years, but geology was not recognized as a scientific endeavor until the 15th century, when a physician named Georgius Agricola developed a logical system for classifying minerals. The formulation of three major principles of modern geology—superposition, original horizontality, and lateral continuity—by Danish priest Nicolaus Steno greatly advanced the field during the 17th century. Elaborator of the principle of uniformitarianism, James Hutton, explained the shape of the Earth as a result of repeated cycles of degradation and sedimentation, leading to the formation of new strata, followed by violent volcanic upheavals. Alexander von Humboldt was a natural philosopher who, at the turn of the 19th century, explored virtually unknown geographic regions seeking natural laws that would relate the Earth's structure, its climate, and its inhabitants. Though he was trained in geology and mineralogy and worked as a mining inspector, he strived for unification of all the branches of natural science. In the early 1800s, French paleontologist Georges Cuvier examined stratigraphical columns in the Paris basin and concluded that sudden breaks represented geological catastrophes in Earth's history that caused the extinction of species. At the same time, self-taught English surveyor William Smith noted that rock beds that shared features such as the same texture, composition, and color also contained similar fossil species, and he utilized this information to create the world's first geological map. The publishing of the influential text *Principles of Geology*, written by Charles Lyell, thrust uniformitarianism into the mainstream and taught geologists how to learn about the past from carefully observing the present. Alfred Wegener agitated the field when he proposed that the continents were not stable but drifted over the surface of the globe. Though he presented geological, climatological, paleontological, paleomagnetic, and biological evidence, Earth scientists were hesitant to accept such an outlandish theory until three decades later when Harry Hammond Hess proposed seafloor spreading as a reasonable mechanism. English geophysicist Arthur Holmes faced skepticism when he tried to convince his colleagues that radiometric dating was the most reliable method for estimating the age of the Earth. More recently, American paleontologist Stephen Jay Gould developed the theory of punctuated equilibrium to explain the lack of intermediate forms in the fossil record and went further to restructure the theory of evolution by natural selection.

Scientists today continue to seek answers about the marvelous events that occurred on this Earth millions and billions of years before the existence of beings with the intelligence and capability to formulate the questions. Though direct observation cannot reveal the answers, Mother Earth has graciously exposed herself in a variety of unique ways, through earthquakes and volcanism, as well as milder but more incessant processes such as weathering and erosion. Because of the advancements brought about by the pioneers profiled in this book, Earth scientists have identified many of the puzzle pieces and now only need to figure out how to piece them together to reveal the Earth's oldest secrets.

Georgius Agricola

(1494–1555)

Georgius Agricola is considered the father of mineralogy. (*Science Photo Library/Photo Researchers, Inc.*)

The Forefather of Geology and the Father of Mineralogy

A long time ago, someone thought it would be useful to develop a *mineral* classification system based on physical properties. This man was a 16th-century physician who called himself Georgius Agricola. His efforts resulted in the inauguration of geology as a science. Geology is the scientific study of the origin, history, and structure of the Earth. Agricola is responsible for organizing the foundation knowledge in the geological subfields of *mineralogy, mining* engineering, physical geology, and *paleontology*. His major works included *De natura fossilum* (On the nature of fossils), which outlined the first mineral classification system based on physical properties, and *De re metallica* (On metallurgy), a comprehensive survey of mining, *metallurgy*, and economic geology of the time. Both of Agricola's books were standard references for over 200 years. In addition, as a physician Agricola was one of the first to recognize occupational hazards.

"Peasant Farmer"

Georg Bauer was born to Gregor Bauer on March 24, 1494, in Glauchau, Germany. His mother's name is unknown. Gregor was a dyer and woolen draper. Not much is recorded of Georg's early life, but he is known to have had at least one older and one younger brother. Georg attended local schools as an adolescent and entered the University of Leipzig in 1514, when he was 20 years old. Most students entered as young teens back then, so he was considered an older student. He received a bachelor's degree the following year but remained at the university as an elementary Greek lecturer. He also continued studying the classics and philosophy until 1518, when he began teaching at the Municipal School in Zwickau. While there, he authored his first textbook, *De prima ac simplici institutione grammatica* (On the elements and simple instruction of grammar, 1520). Though he was promoted to the positions equivalent to vice principal and principal, he decided to study medicine and returned to Leipzig to do so.

As was popular at the time, Georg Bauer Latinized his name to Georgius Agricola, meaning "peasant farmer." He is commonly known as Agricola. The Catholic Agricola studied medicine in Italy at the University of Bologna and the University of Padua on a special three-year fellowship from his Zwickau church. In 1526, he was granted his medical degree and married Anna Meiner. During his travels he met the famous Latin scholar and writer Desiderius Erasmus, who became an important figure when Agricola published his first scientific text. Agricola also assisted in the editing of Hippocrates's and Galen's medical writings for the Aldina Press.

An Expert on Mining

Agricola moved to Joachimsthal, in Bohemia (now part of the western Czech Republic), where he served as the town physician and apothecary. An apothecary was similar to a pharmacist. Joachimsthal was a relatively new and rapidly growing silver-mining community and was in need of teachers, preachers, and physicians. Many of the inhabitants of the town suffered from lung disease due to their work in the mines. Agricola felt it was important that he understand the process of mining in order to understand his patients' illnesses. He was also interested in the use of minerals and smelting products for medical treatments. Thus he took it upon himself to learn the business of mining and metallurgy.

Agricola took this self-imposed mission seriously. He learned about every aspect of the business—the technical, the physical, the economic, the medical, and the worker's lifestyles. The book *Bermannus; sive de re metallica dialogues* (Bermannus; or a dialogue on metallurgy, 1530) summarized much of the information he gathered and gave a description of the minerals in Saxon, particularly bismuth. The popular text was written as a conversation between an experienced miner and two philosophers interested in learning about mining. The eminent Erasmus wrote a favorable introduction to the book, assuring its success. As a former scholar of classics, Agricola wrote all of his books in Latin. This was difficult since much mining vocabulary was German-based and made future translations awkward. Agricola's next two important books were political and economic in nature.

As he became well-known as an author, an expert on metallurgy, and a town physician and apothecary, Agricola desired a more peaceful life, so he moved to a smelting community, Chemnitz, in what is now Germany. Once again, he served as town physician. Using his knowledge of mining, he made some valuable investments and became very rich in just a few years. In 1541, his first wife died, and the following year he married Anna Schütz, the daughter of a local guildmaster.

Shortly after his arrival in Chemnitz, Agricola was asked to work as the court historiographer, a task that occupied his time for 20 years. In this capacity he was responsible for researching and docu-

Mining and Metallurgy

Mining is the extraction of solid minerals, or *ores*, from the Earth. Minerals are naturally occurring, nonliving materials of a fixed chemical composition and highly ordered characteristic structure, including gemstones and metals. Ores are mined to obtain their commercially valuable mineral components for making everything from building materials to fine jewelry. Mining is necessary to obtain materials such as iron, *coal*, gold, copper, diamonds, phosphate, and gravel.

Strip mining, open-pit mining, and quarrying are common methods of extracting minerals from deposits near the Earth's surface. While surface

menting the genealogy of the Saxon rulers. His results from this effort were not published until 1963, probably because the rulers were somehow disappointed in his findings, specifically, the lack of finding that they were heirs to additional territories. Duke Maurice, elector of Saxony, appointed Agricola burgomaster, or mayor of the city (he served four terms); a councilor to the Saxon court; and ambassador to the Holy Roman Emperor Charles V. It was rare for a Catholic to serve in such an important capacity for a Protestant duke, as the tension between the two faiths was high. At any rate, it seems Agricola's quest for a more peaceful life than he had in Joachimsthal was not very successful. He was forced to set aside his science for a few years.

A Prolific Author

Once he had time to pursue science, he was very prolific. In 1546 he published several texts. *De ortu et causis subterraneorum* (On the emergence of materials from underground) contained many ideas that influenced future geological studies. It is considered the first

techniques are cheaper, underground mining is preferable for deeper deposits or in circumstances in which the amount of waste material that must be removed to extract ore is too large. Unlike in Agricola's time, today, safety for underground miners is paramount; air vents provide fresh air, noxious gases and dangerous dusts are removed, and roofs are supported. Wells are used to mine for liquid or gaseous materials.

After mining, metal ores are often sent to industrial facilities called *smelters* to produce crude metal products that are then refined into a purer state. Metallurgy is the science and technology of extracting metals from their ores, of purifying metals, and of creating useful items from metals. Metallurgy can be subdivided into two categories: extractive and physical. Extractive metallurgy includes removal of metals from their ores and purifying them, whereas physical metallurgy is concerned with adapting the metal for its final use.

textbook on physical geology. In it, Agricola criticized supernatural explanations for geological formations and emphasized the effects of *erosion* by wind and water. He also discussed the effect of Earth's internal heat on volcanoes and earthquakes. Agricola proposed that mountains were formed from winds moving sand, subterranean winds, earthquakes, volcanic fires, and water erosion. The term *lapidifying juice* was introduced to describe the versatile, mineral-laden liquids exuded by the Earth. He suggested that ore deposits originated from such solutions of dissolved minerals that filtered into the cracks of *rocks*, forming mineral *veins*. That same year he also published works on water and gases that existed below the Earth's surface, underground creatures, and a history and summary of the ancient geographical distribution of metals.

De natura fossilum (1546) earned Agricola the title father of modern mineralogy. Mineralogy is the study of the distribution, identification, and properties of minerals. At the time, the term *fossil* implied anything that was dug from the ground, including minerals and gemstones, as well as what are referred to today as fossils, remnants of organisms from the past. The book included a summary of previous works on minerals and offered the first attempt at mineral classification based on physical properties rather than by irrelevant characteristics such as proposed magical uses. He outlined a system based on properties such as shape, color, solubility, hardness, density, combustibility, and texture. The descriptions he gave of different minerals were very detailed. In this text, he also made an attempt to differentiate between simple *elements* and *compounds*. Today, mineral classification is based on chemical analyses as well as X-ray diffraction and isotopic analysis, so current students might not be impressed by Agricola's ingenuity. However, one must remember that modern chemistry knowledge or methodology did not yet exist. Agricola noted the similarities of many fossils to living organisms but did not pursue this suggestion vigorously.

Agricola published other books in 1549 and 1550 that discussed the origins of rocks, mountains, and volcanoes. At that point he visited Joachimsthal for several weeks. He was very disturbed by the destruction of the once thriving town, mostly due to poor governing. Being financially well-off, he assisted in the economic recovery of the town by generously donating a large sum of money to be used for the search of new deposits to mine.

The Black Death struck Saxony in the early 1550s. The plague was caused by bacteria and spread by flea-infested rats. Infected victims developed fevers and swollen *lymph* nodes. The mortality rates reached 75 percent, and death occurred only days after the initial disease symptoms appeared. Agricola worked very hard day and night treating his patients and lost his own daughter to the disease. He published *De peste* (On the plague) in 1554, describing his observations and studies on the plague.

On Metallurgy

Of all Agricola accomplished in his life, *De re metallica*, published four months after he passed away, was his culminating legacy. As a greatly expanded version of his book *Bermannus; sive de re metallica dialogues*, it mostly discussed mining and metallurgy, including all minerals. He explained the geology of ores; methods for *surveying*; how mines were constructed, pumped, and ventilated; and the equipment miners used. He also discussed the methods for assaying ores, transportation

Mining equipment. This woodcut illustration from *De re metallica* shows a water wheel powering a pulley mechanism above a mine shaft: A) axle, B) wheel that is turned by treading, C) toothed wheel, D) drum made of rundles, E) drum to which are fixed iron clamps, F) second wheel, and G) balls. *(Library of Congress, Prints and Photographs Division [LC-USZ62-76201])*

Mining methods. This woodcut illustration from *De re metallica* shows men chopping wood, damming a stream, and washing ore to obtain stones from which tin is made. A) stream, B) ditch, C) mattock, D) pieces of turf, E) seven-pronged fork, F) iron shovel, G) trough, H) another trough, and I) small, wooden trowel. *(Library of Congress, Prints and Photographs Division [LC-USZ62-95282])*

of ores, preparation for smelting, and the processes of smelting and refining. The text surveyed the location and content of ancient mines. He described laws governing mining, ownership of mines, and the business aspect of mines and also recorded his observation of the ordered, layered appearance of rocks, another important contribution to geology. He suggested that though ores were deposited inside some rocks, the rocks containing them were older than the ores themselves—the ores had been deposited into cracks in the rocks by solutions containing dissolved minerals. Predicting the future importance of chemical analysis in metallurgy, he included a section describing current chemical technology. Lastly, sections on glass-making and the chemicals used in smelting were incorporated. This text is also famous for its illustrations, whose woodcuts were used for over a century in seven editions.

The religious struggle between the Protestant and the Catholic faiths escalated in the mid-16th century. When Agricola died on November 21, 1555, the Protestants and Catholics argued over his burial. The Protestants did not want the Catholic man's remains buried in the Chemnitz parish church, an honor usually bestowed upon former mayors. An old friend who was a bishop intervened to allow interment at the Zeitz cathedral.

In the preface to *De re metallica*, Agricola emphasized the importance of relying on observation rather than speculation. This was a practice by which he lived, and in doing so, he converted mineralogy from an occupation into a scientific discipline. The days of divining rods, magic crystals, and thunderstones were on their way out. Agricola may not have been appreciated fully during his lifetime, as his writing was difficult to decipher and translate, but his works brought about the commencement of the geological sciences. Progress in the fields of mineralogy and metallurgy could only follow after a massive undertaking of the descriptions of the current knowledge and techniques.

CHRONOLOGY

1494	Georgius Agricola is born on March 24 in Glauchau, Germany
1514–18	Studies at the University of Leipzig

1518–22	Teaches Latin and Greek at a school in Zwickau
1520	Writes first work, *De prima ac simplici institutione grammatica* (On the elements and simple instruction of grammar)
1523–26	Studies medicine at the Universities of Bologna and Padua in Italy
Early 1520s	Works at Aldina Press
1527–33	Serves as the town physician in Joachimsthal
1530	Publishes *Bermannus; sive de re metallica dialogues* (Bermannus; or a dialogue on metallurgy)
1531–33	Publishes books on economics and politics
1533	Begins working as the town physician in Chemnitz
1534–54	Serves as court historiographer
1546	Agricola is appointed mayor of Chemnitz and diplomatic representative to the Holy Roman Emperor Charles V. He publishes *De ortu et causis subterraneorum* (On the emergence of materials from underground) and *De natura fossilum* (On the nature of fossils).
1554	Publishes *De peste* (On the plague)
1555	Dies on November 21 in Chemnitz
1556	*De re metallica* (On metallurgy) is published posthumously

FURTHER READING

Dibner, Bern. *Agricola on Metals*. Norwalk, Conn.: Burndy Library, 1958. Describes the history and development of technology for metallurgy and mining ores.

Gillispie, Charles C., ed. *Dictionary of Scientific Biography*. Vol. 1. New York: Scribner, 1970–76. Good source for facts concerning personal backgrounds and scientific accomplishments but assumes reader has basic knowledge of science.

Olson, Richard, ed. *Biographical Encyclopedia of Scientists.* Vol. 1. New York: Marshall Cavendish, 1998. Contains brief biographies including timelines of significant events.

Simonis, Doris A., ed. *Lives and Legacies: Scientists, Mathematicians, and Inventors.* Phoenix, Ariz.: Oryx Press, 1999. Contains one-page profiles.

University of California–Berkeley Museum of Paleontology. "Georgius Agricola (1494–1555)." Available online. URL: http://www.ucmp.berkeley.edu/history/agricola.html. Accessed January 14, 2005. Standard biography with related links.

Nicolaus Steno

(1638–1686)

Nicolaus Steno is considered the father of geology. *(Science Photo Library/Photo Researchers, Inc.)*

The Law of Superposition of Rock Layers and the Principles of Original Horizontality and Lateral Extension

Nicolaus Steno was a sort of detective who figured out the history of the Earth from clues left behind over billions of years. He believed that the Earth revealed its historical secrets in the structure of its geological *strata*, or horizontal layers of rock. Though he began his scientific career as a proficient anatomist, Steno is fittingly labeled the father of geology for formulating in a single geological work three major principles: the law of *superposition*, the principle of *original horizontality*, and the principle of lateral continuity. After laying down these basic laws for the new field of geology, he quit science and devoted the rest of his life to serving Catholic missions in northern Europe.

An Interest in Science

Niels Stensen was born on January 1, 1638, to Sten Pedersen and Anne Nielsdatter in Copenhagen, Denmark. Sten was a skilled goldsmith, and one of his regular customers was the Danish king. Though the king was lax about paying his bills, the Sten Pedersen household lived comfortably. Niels suffered from an unknown illness from the age of three to six. As he recovered, his father died, leaving the family without a source of income. Anne remarried quickly, but her new husband died the following year. She did marry again, but Niels's childhood was quite unstable, foreshadowing the rest of his life. In addition, the mid-1600s was a rough period for Denmark. The Thirty Years' War had ravaged Europe since 1618. Catholics and Protestants clashed over rights and doctrines. Between 1654 and 1655, the plague stole the lives of one-third of the Danish population.

In the midst of all this, Niels received an education. He attended the Lutheran academy Vor Frue Skole, which lost half its student population to the plague. As was common for educated people at the time, his name was Latinized to Nicolai Stenosis, which has since been altered to Nicolaus Steno. Ole Borch taught Steno Latin at Vor Frue, but Borch was interested in many subjects and was also an admired physician. He is credited with pointing Steno toward science. He performed many scientific demonstrations that impressed Steno. The two men developed a friendship based on a common love of natural and experimental philosophy.

Steno entered the University of Copenhagen in 1656 to study medicine. It was an unfortunate time to attend college because the country went to war with Sweden. Food and fuel were in short supply on campus. Many professors and fellow students joined the war effort, leaving numbers behind essentially to teach themselves. This was not a problem for Steno, who read voraciously. During this time, he kept a journal titled *Chaos*. Much of what is known about Steno's studies, inner struggles, personal characteristics, and reflections on literature were recorded in this journal.

The Seashell Question

Thomas Bartholin, an *anatomy* professor from the University of Copenhagen, was famous for his discovery of the vessels that carry lymph throughout the body. Lymph is a transparent, yellowish fluid that plays an important role in the immune system and in the transportation of certain materials throughout the body. Bartholin was a fashionable lecturer but had retired just before Steno entered the university. Nevertheless, the two made each other's acquaintance, and Bartholin conveyed not only an appreciation for anatomy to Steno, but also introduced the famous seashell question to him.

In mountainous regions, objects which resembled seashells and other marine life-forms were found embedded in the rock of the mountains. Though their shape resembled that of marine life, their composition was of a different material, more similar to hardened rock than brittle shells. Did they grow naturally out of the Earth itself? Or might they be remains of past marine life? One thing on which Catholics and Protestants did agree was the creation of the Earth and all life by an omnipotent God, but land and water were separated on the third day of creation, whereas fowl and water life were created on the fifth day. So, if the fossils were the remains of past marine life, how did they get to be embedded in dry land? (At the time the word *fossil* referred to anything that came from the Earth.) One possible explanation was the great flood described in Genesis. However, given the short period the entire Earth was covered by water, there was not enough time for slow clams to travel the distance to the remote locations where the fossils were sometimes found. Besides, they were made of a different material. The arguments went back and forth. This paradox bothered some people more than others. Steno listened to Bartholin's debate with intrigue and recorded several notes about fossils in his *Chaos* journal; nonetheless, he continued with his medical studies. He was particularly interested in anatomy.

Steno originally had wanted to study mathematics, but medicine offered better prospects for a career. Anatomy seemed very clear and logical to Steno. Perhaps it appeased his mathematical yearnings. After three years at Copenhagen, Steno left for the Netherlands in possession of a letter of introduction from Bartholin. He stopped by Amsterdam and was hosted by a physician friend of Bartholin's, Gerhard Bläes. In Amsterdam, Bläes gave Steno private anatomy lessons.

Discovery of a Salivary Duct

One day Steno was examining the arteries and veins surrounding the jaws on a butchered sheep head. He inserted his metal probe through an opening and suddenly heard a clinking noise from hitting teeth. After close examination, he realized he had discovered a previously unrecognized duct leading from the parotid glands to the oral cavity. The parotid glands supply saliva to the mouth. He pointed this out to his teacher. Bläes immediately dismissed Steno's finding as a blunder. He thought Steno must have accidentally probed through the side of the sheep's cheek, but Steno had faith in his dissecting skills. When he demonstrated to Bläes that he did not puncture the cheek, Bläes retorted that it must be a deformity.

After staying in Amsterdam for three months, Steno made his way to Leiden, where he enrolled at the university in 1660. He repeated his dissection to his new professors, who excitedly accepted the duct as a new and real discovery. They presented his findings. Word got back to Amsterdam, and Bläes angrily responded that it was his own discovery and that Steno had stolen credit. Bläes rushed to publish his account of the newly discovered duct. This must have frustrated Steno to no end. He knew Bläes made a bogus claim, but who was he to publicly argue against the famous anatomist? So Steno worked extra hard to prove his skills as an anatomist. He continued his dissection studies and, in 1662, published *Anatomical Observations on Glands*, in which he described not only the parotids but all of the glands in the head. He built up a highly regarded reputation and was able to reveal the inaccuracies of Bläes's report by providing a description that only an extremely skilled anatomist could give. Bläes must have been very embarrassed by Steno's triumph and jealous of his future successes. The duct leading from the parotids to the oral cavity is referred to today as Stensen's duct, *ductus stenosis.*

When his stepfather died in 1663, Steno briefly returned to Copenhagen. In 1664, he published the results of his years of research at Leiden, *On Muscles and Glands.* That same year Steno was awarded a doctorate of medicine from the University of Leiden in absentia. He was hopeful of obtaining a position at the University of Copenhagen but was rejected. Thus he set out again, landing in Paris for a year.

Questioning Descartes

Steno believed the best way to learn was to study objects of interest directly. For example, to understand poetry one should not simply read one scholar's interpretations of a verse but read the verse himself or herself. If one was curious about botany, he or she should observe plants in addition to looking at pictures in books. Though Steno was well-read, he did not believe books were the utmost authority. Proof was necessary for progress. The 17th-century French philosopher and mathematician René Descartes had popularized the method of systemically doubting everything at first. Direct observation or other reliable proof was necessary to attain absolute certainty. The young Dane subscribed to this new philosophy.

By 1665, Steno was engrossed in the anatomy of the brain. Though much had been written about the structure and function of the brain, Steno confessed at a public lecture in Paris to knowing nothing about the organ. After shocking the audience by making such a bold declaration, the prominent anatomist proceeded to explain his philosophy on learning. He said he was starting from scratch. Rather than relying on the varied, written descriptions from centuries of so-called anatomists who had mangled brains and followed only prescribed methods of dissection, he planned to explore it carefully on his own. He would accept only that which he directly observed. His presentation, *Discourse on the Anatomy of the*

Brain, is remembered for his scientific philosophy as well as the content itself.

Steno had been initially introduced to Cartesian philosophy by Ole Borch. While Steno subscribed to Descartes's method of doubting first, he was bothered by Descartes's lack of practicing what he preached. For example, the function of the heart had mystified physicians for centuries. The ancient Greek philosopher Aristotle believed the heart was responsible for a person's emotions and intelligence. In the second century, Galen said the heart was the body's source of heat and that it was the seat of the soul. It prepared "vital spirits" that were transported around the body in the blood, giving life to the organism. Descartes said the heart was a furnace. When the blood passed through it, it became heated and expanded, and as a result, the blood rushed into the arteries. Back in Leiden, Steno had been intrigued by this view and decided to investigate. He purchased an ox heart from the local butcher. He cooked the

Cartesian Philosophy

French mathematician René Descartes (1596–1650) is considered a founder of modern philosophy. Descartes also invented analytic geometry, in which geometrical analysis is used to solve algebraic problems, and algebra is used to solve geometrical problems. He published three major works: *Discourse on the Method of Rightly Conducting One's Reason, and Seeking Truth in the Sciences* (1637), *Meditations on First Philosophy* (1641), and *Principles of Philosophy* (1644). As a philosopher, he desired an explanation for all the world's phenomena, but he was frustrated with traditional philosophical and theological methods.

In his *Discourse on Method,* Descartes attempted to incorporate the methods of logic and mathematics into his philosophy. He thought sci-

organ and carefully peeled away the outer protective layer, noticing fibers similar to those present in muscle tissue. The fibers were arranged in a manner such that contraction would force the blood out through the arteries. Having a rabbit on hand, he dissected its muscles to compare to the ox's heart. Not surprisingly, he found them to be essentially the same. He concluded that the heart was simply a muscle that worked to pump blood around the body. Sometimes things are as simple as they seem. Yet this instance troubled him, and he began losing faith in Cartesian philosophy. He brought these doubts with him from Amsterdam to Paris.

In *On Man*, Descartes claimed that the human body was simply a machine and that the pineal gland coordinated movements of the body in accordance with the feelings of the soul. He thought the pineal gland caused the actual moving by pulling strings like a puppeteer. It seemed that Descartes based an awful lot of assumptions either on shoddy dissections or the inaccurate records of others. In

entific knowledge needed to be built from scratch rather than simply adding to the old, and he provided rules for doing so. The most important tenet was accepting as true only propositions whose truth was so clear and distinct that there was no occasion for doubt. The systematic process of doubting became a conviction of modern science as the Scientific Revolution approached.

Descartes was a master of epistemology, the study of the nature and origin of knowledge. He emphasized the need to doubt everything, believing knowledge required absolute certainty. Everything he previously thought he knew was derived from potentially erroneous logic or derived from his senses and therefore must be called into question. This led him to trust that the only certainty was the existence of himself as a thinking being. The famous phrase *"Cogito, ergo sum"* (I think, therefore I am) was first pronounced by Descartes in *Meditations on First Philosophy*. He meant that because he was capable of thinking and doubting, he must exist, because someone had to be doing the thinking.

his Parisian brain dissections, Steno found the pineal gland to be completely stationary. There was no way it could perform the functions Descartes claimed. Cartesian anatomy seemed to be based on faulty deductive reasoning and conjecture rather than experimentation. Steno was extremely disturbed by this conclusion.

How could one accept Descartes's rational proof of the existence of God when Descartes could not even verify basic anatomical facts? From *Chaos*, it is known that Steno was always deeply religious, but this sequence of events caused him much spiritual anxiety. Nevertheless, he stood by the mechanical approach to science, even if Descartes had not. He became frustrated with Paris, where people did not want to hear him question the venerated Descartes. So he picked up and moved again.

Studies on Muscular Contraction

In 1666, he arrived in Florence, Italy, by way of the Alps, where he was reminded of the seashell question. He was awed by the massive mountains and delighted to observe the rock strata firsthand. He was also pleased to find a group of similar-minded philosophers who thrived on experimental science. One of these men was Francesco Redi, the grand duke's physician. Redi had disproved spontaneous generation. People had thought that flies came to life from dung or rotting meat, but Redi showed that if the meat was covered with netting, then no flies appeared. Preexisting flies needed access to the organic matter to lay the eggs that developed into maggots. Redi was a member of the Accademia del Cimento, a group devoted to experimental science. This group was sponsored by the grand duke of Tuscany, Ferdinando II de'Medici, and his brother Prince Leopoldo. The intelligent Medici brothers were not only formal philanthropists, but also active participators in the experiments and discussions of the Cimento. They generously provided materials for experiments and welcomed Steno into their association. The grand duke gave him an appointment as a physician at the Hospital of Santa Maria Nuova, leaving him plenty of time to pursue independent research.

Steno had been working on a new line of research involving muscle contraction. Anatomists believed that muscles moved because something pushed on them, yet muscles seemed to contract on their own. How did this happen? It certainly was not the pineal gland. One hypothesis was that fluids rushed in, causing the muscle to swell. With support from other members of the Cimento, Steno pursued this problem. Geometrically, he showed that when a muscle contracted, it neither grew nor shrunk. The overall volume was maintained though the shape of the muscle fibers changed by contracting. These results were published in *Elements of Muscular Knowledge* in 1667.

Glossopetrae

While waiting for these results to be published in fall 1666, an enormous great white shark that weighed about 2,800 pounds (1,270 kg) was captured and killed on a beach near Livorno. Ferdinando asked Steno to dissect its head, which was brought to Florence. Before a large audience, Steno carefully dissected the skin and soft tissues and examined the nerves and tiny brain. The excitement at the scene must have been incredulous. The beast's teeth were almost three inches (7.6 cm) long, and each jaw had 13 rows, but the shape of the teeth was what drew Steno's attention. They resembled a type of fossil about which he had first learned from Bartholin and had since viewed for himself. *Glossopetrae*, sometimes called tongue stones, were a type of hard, blackish, serrated, triangular stone. They were believed to have magical powers and were used to treat everything from speech impediments to poisoning. No one knew exactly where they came from. Some thought they were hardened woodpecker tongues. Others thought they fell from the heavens. They seemed abundant after heavy rain, so maybe they were jagged edges from lightning bolts. One explanation was biblical. The apostle Paul had been bitten by a poisonous snake on the island of Malta but was unaffected by the bite. The Maltese people thought Paul cursed the viper, making its venom harmless, and that nature honored this miracle by growing the glossopetrae in the shape of viper's teeth. Steno thought they looked suspiciously similar to shark teeth.

He questioned all the stories he had heard and became obsessed with determining the nature of these glossopetrae. Steno was not the first to compare the tongue stones to shark teeth, but if they were shark teeth, how did they get onto dry land? And why was their composition different from live shark teeth? These questions reminded him of the seashell paradox. Actually, the marine bodies found in the Earth were often very near the glossopetrae. But the popular belief was that they came from the Earth itself. The Earth contained lapidifying juices (mineral-laden solutions) and unexplained "plastic forces" that gave form where none existed previously. People claimed that they could almost see rocks and other inanimate objects grow and multiply on pathways and in fields. The fact that some of the fossils resembled current marine creatures was a trick of nature.

Steno began his examination. He compared glossopetrae side by side with shark teeth and found they were the same. Most of the arguments supporting the spontaneous growth theory were easily dismissed through logical reasoning. He described anatomical evidence supporting his belief. He explained that the chemical composition could change during fossilization, though the shape would be preserved. He very cautiously worded his report to the grand duke, timidly stating that one would not be so far from the truth in saying the glossopetrae might be fossilized shark teeth.

He was mentally engaged deep in the Earth following his preliminary studies and wanted to continue studying natural history. Just as the structure of body parts divulged their function, he believed the structure of the Earth also had something to say. Now he wondered not only how the seashell got on the mountaintop but how the mountain itself got there. Rather than rely on past speculation or biblical stories, he figured that studying the Earth was a good place to start finding certain truths about its own history. He was still deeply religious but began applying his critical thinking to his own religious beliefs. Whereas the Lutherans believed the Bible should be literally accepted, the Catholics were more lenient. After spending time observing the nature surrounding him, Steno had a hard time accepting that creation took place over only several days. What he observed from the Earth, its strata, the mountains, and the fossils told a different story.

The fact that the shapes of some fossils were true to the original forms of some current marine creatures told him that the shells must have been laid in a soft muddy layer that molded around the

Stratification is very apparent in this photograph taken from Yavapai Point at Grand Canyon National Park, Arizona. *(Courtesy of C. A. Edwards, U.S. Geological Survey)*

around the shell. Other subsequent events led to the hardening of the *sediment* while preserving the original shape. A solid became enclosed in another solid. He carried this further. Noting the ordered horizontal layering of the Earth's strata, he said that the layers must have resulted from sediment settling at the bottom of a liquid. The liquid evenly spread out across the surface, and the minerals and particles contained within the liquid fell heaviest first over the surface of the preceding layer. Also, each layer spread out continuously over the Earth's surface, except where other large solid structures impeded the flow of the liquid. Furthermore, the layer underneath must have solidified before the upper layer hardened. This process occurred repeatedly, with each layer containing within it pieces of history from that geological age. Steno believed this took much longer than the 6,000 years that the Earth was believed to be in existence based on a biblical chronology. Scientists have since determined the Earth to be about 4.6 billion years old. Steno published some of his findings along with his shark head dissection report in 1667. The report was added as an addendum to his muscle paper, which was still at the printer from the previous fall.

A Forerunner

Impressed, the grand duke granted him a salary, and Steno became a full member of the Cimento. He was able to explore fully his new geological interests with all expenses paid. He traveled around Tuscany collecting fossils, climbing mountains, and examining strata. He also continued dabbling in anatomy and arrived at a startling conclusion. It was obvious that females of many *species* of animals laid eggs, but Steno proved that females that gave birth to live organisms also produced eggs in their ovaries. This was important because people generally believed that the female only acted as an incubator for the seed that the man placed inside of her. However, most of Steno's time was spent deciphering the history of the Earth as told by its anatomy; that is, its distinct and unique geological formations.

Steno was thoroughly enjoying his scientific freedom and making remarkable progress. Unfortunately, in fall 1667, three events had a profound effect on the direction his life would soon take. First, Leopoldo was elected a cardinal and would no longer be able to manage the Cimento. Second, Steno received a letter from the king of Denmark requesting he return home and offering him a decent salary. Lastly, Steno converted to Catholicism. This would not please the Danish king, as Catholicism was banned in Denmark. Thus Steno wrote a letter to the king in reply explaining his religious conversion.

Previously, he would have been thrilled at being given such a position, but Denmark could not provide the rich geological material for his research that Italy could. He felt his new studies were coming to an end. He hastily continued observing shells and strata and crystals. By 1668, he started writing up his interpretations, *De solido intra solidum naturaliter contento dissertationis prodromus* (Forerunner to a dissertation on solids naturally enclosed in solids). This work is commonly referred to as *Prodromus* and was Steno's magnum opus that earned him the title founder of geology. The full dissertation never materialized, but *Prodromus* was packed full of clearly explained rational ideas, setting the framework for the new science of geology.

The principles outlined in *Prodromus* truly set the stage for all future geological studies. In attempting to address the central question of how a solid becomes enclosed in another solid, Steno revealed three chief geological principles. The law of superposition stated that the layers of strata in the Earth's *crust* represent a relative geological chronology. Each layer of *sedimentary rock* was older than the one above it and younger than the one below it. When a layer formed, all the matter on top of it was still fluid, and the layer below it was already hardened. The principle of original horizontality maintained that the layers of sediment were leveled after

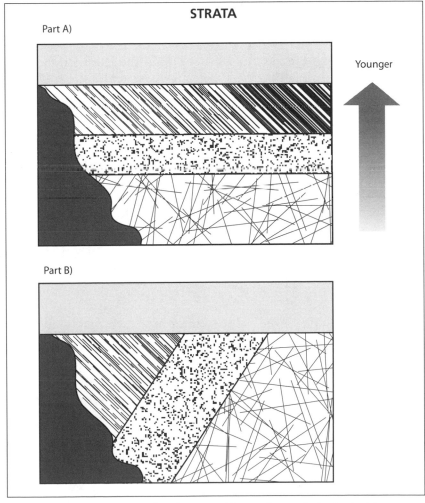

Sediments are deposited in flat, horizontal layers (part A). Geological forces may tilt the original formation (part B).

being deposited by water and to a lesser effect, wind. If strata lie positioned at an angle, it was the result of a calamitous event that disrupted the crustal arrangement after the deposition. For example, a volcanic eruption or strong water current could cause a disturbance in an ordered stratigraphic sequence. The principal of *lateral extension* stated that strata were encompassed on all sides, or completely extended around the spherical Earth. Though these principles might seem quite simple today, Steno was the first to clearly state them. Steno also noticed that in crystal formation, the angles between the faces of the crystals were constant regardless of the shape or size of the crystal. This is referred to as the law of angle constancy.

In those days, books could not be published until they were approved by censors. The first *Prodromus* censor, Vincenzo Viviani, gave it a favorable recommendation. The second one, Redi, was more conservative and withheld it for several months. In the meantime, Steno received a reply from the king of Denmark granting him a position as royal anatomist in Copenhagen. A professorship was out of the question since he was now a Catholic. Steno left the arrangements for publication of *Prodromus* to Viviani and returned to Copenhagen for two years. They were not happy years. His research and spirit suffered, prompting him to request a leave from the king so he could return to Florence, which he did in 1674.

Devotion to Catholic Missions

The new grand duke hired Steno to tutor his 11-year-old son. Then in 1675, Steno was ordained and took a vow of poverty. The pope appointed him a bishop in 1677. For the remainder of his life he lived ascetically and served missions in northern Germany, Denmark, and Norway. He worked on behalf of the poor and homeless and tried to increase interest in the priesthood. Many Protestants converted to Catholicism under Steno's influence.

The last years of his life were fairly dismal. In 1684, he wrote to the pope, pleading for a release from his obligations. He wanted to return to Florence, where his days had been happiest. He was officially granted his request, but right before leaving he was asked to make a detour to help strengthen a new church in Schwerin. Unfortunately, the priest whom Steno was to be helping became ill, and Steno's brief delay in northern Germany was extended two years.

Steno became more and more extreme with regard to his self-denial and sacrifice. He even sold his bishop's ring and cross and gave the money away. Years of overwork, sleep deprivation, fasting, and not taking care of his physical needs took its toll, and Steno himself fell gravely ill. Diagnosed with gallstones, his middle became so swollen that he thought his abdomen would split open. He called for a priest to come administer his last sacraments, but he knew he would not make it in time. So he made a public confession to his household and asked a devoted disciple whom he had converted to Catholicism to read him prayers for the sick and the dead. He died at age 48, on November 25, 1686, in Schwerin. His only belongings were a few worn-out garments.

Steno was not buried until 11 months later. His body was shipped from Hamburg to Florence in a crate that supposedly contained books. Seamen would have been hesitant to transport the crate if they had known its true contents. Steno's remains were buried in the crypt of the Medici in the San Lorenzo church.

Three hundred years after Steno's birth, a group of Danish pilgrims nominated Steno for canonization as a saint. In 1953, Steno's remains were transferred to a small chapel where there was also an altar available. Pope Pius XI began the process of gathering information proving his sanctity. Proof of one miraculous healing event earned Steno beatification, one step short of canonization, by Pope John Paul II on October 23, 1988. Steno's scientific career was brief, but his *Prodromus* is as relevant today as it was when it was published over 300 years ago, and his ideas are presented in all current basic geology textbooks. In honor of the 300-year anniversary of the publication of *Prodromus*, in 1969, the Danish Geological Society started awarding a Steno Medal for outstanding achievements in the field of geology.

Steno's greatness was in clearly and formally stating that which seems simple and obvious, though it stirred up controversy at the time. People did not want to believe the heart, the seat of the soul, was simply a muscle. And what was fantastical about the organic material of shark teeth being replaced with mineral matter? Most upsetting, however, was Steno's insistence that scientists look to the Earth itself rather than supernatural revelation to learn about its creation. It took a frail Danish priest to open up the field of geology by reading a story that had been waiting to be told for billions of years.

CHRONOLOGY

1638	Niels Stensen (Nicolaus Steno) is born on January 1 in Copenhagen, Denmark
1648	Begins attending the Vor Frue School
1656–59	Studies medicine at the University of Copenhagen
1660	Discovers the duct of the parotid glands
1660–63	Studies at the University of Leiden
1662	Publishes *Anatomical Observations*
1664	Publishes *On Muscles and Glands* and receives a medical degree from the University of Leiden in absentia
1665	Presents *Discourse on the Anatomy of the Brain* in Paris (published in 1669)
1666	Dissects a shark head
1667	Publishes *Elements of Muscular Knowledge,* including his shark head dissection report as an addendum, and converts to Catholicism
1668	Receives a summons from the Danish king to return to Denmark
1669	Publishes *Prodromus,* articulating the law of superposition, the principle of original horizontality, and the principle of lateral extension
1672	Arrives in Copenhagen to serve as royal anatomist

1674–76	Returns to Florence and tutors the crown prince
1677	Is consecrated as bishop for the northern missions
1677–86	Serves the northern European Catholic missions
1686	Dies at age 48 on November 25 in Schwerin, Germany
1988	Pope John Paul II beatifies Steno

FURTHER READING

Cloud, Preston. *Adventures in Earth History; being a volume of significant writings from original sources, on cosmology, geology, climatology, oceanography, organic evolution, and related topics of interest to students of earth history, from the time of Nicolaus Steno to the present.* San Francisco, Calif.: W. H. Freeman, 1970. Includes original articles of pioneering research in the Earth sciences.

Cutler, Alan. *The Seashell on the Mountaintop: A Story of Science, Sainthood and the Humble Genius Who Discovered a New History of the Earth.* New York: Dutton, 2003. The most complete biography of Steno's life. Enjoyable story.

Gillispie, Charles C., ed. *Dictionary of Scientific Biography.* Vol. 13. New York: Scribner, 1970–76. Good source for facts concerning personal backgrounds and scientific accomplishments but assumes reader has basic knowledge of science.

University of California–Berkeley Museum of Paleontology. "Nicholas Steno (1638–1686)." Available online. URL: http://www.ucmp.berkeley.edu/history/steno.html. Accessed January 15, 2005. Standard biography.

James Hutton

(1726–1797)

James Hutton is considered a pioneer in geology for formulating the principle of uniformitarianism. *(Science Photo Library/Photo Researchers, Inc.)*

Uniformitarianism as the Central Principle of Historical Geology

In the 18th century, a young man devoted his life to studying the Earth and the processes by which it was shaped. James Hutton was a major theorist of his time, but his fame as a pioneer in the Earth sciences rests upon a single work. He proposed a system for shaping the surface of the Earth. He believed the chief agent for major geological changes was heat generated deep underneath the Earth's crust. Proponents of Hutton's theory of the Earth were called *vulcanists*—after Vulcan, the Roman god of fire, due to the emphasis of his system on the action of heat and volcanoes—or *plutonists*, after the ruler of the underworld, Pluto. Hutton's proposal of a continuously acting cyclical system of degradation of the land into sediment that was deposited into strata under the sea, followed by upheaval from volcanic activity, led to decades of debate.

A Lawyer's Apprentice

James Hutton was the son of William Hutton and Sarah Balfour. He was born in Edinburgh, Scotland, on June 3, 1726. William died when James was only three. He had been a successful merchant and the city treasurer and had good control of his family's finances. The inheritance he left was sufficient for Sarah to raise James and his three sisters and to send James to the University of Edinburgh when he was 14 years old. While in college, James studied humanities, but he became particularly interested in chemistry when a professor performed an experiment demonstrating that a single acid could dissolve inferior metals but that two acids were necessary to dissolve gold.

Despite showing promising academic potential and natural intellectual curiosity, James began an apprenticeship in a lawyer's office when he was 17 years old; however, it was obvious to everyone that James's interests lay elsewhere. His boss took pity on him and released him from their agreement. Because coursework in medicine offered the most opportunity to learn chemistry, James enrolled in medical school at the University of Edinburgh. After three years there, he moved to Paris to study anatomy. In 1749, he was awarded a doctor of medicine degree after transferring to Leiden, but he was not interested in practicing medicine.

Geological and Agricultural Studies

James traveled a little, and his interest in chemistry grew into a love of geology and mineralogy. Between 1752 and 1753, he lived with a farmer in Norfolk, England, where he was fascinated by the rows of black *flints* embedded in the white *chalk*. He spent time gazing at heaps of seashells on the east coast and noticed chalk and foreign stones embedded in cliffs to the north. In the west he observed red-colored chalk in the strata. With such geological variety above-ground, he wondered what was underneath the ground.

Hutton also gained practical knowledge of agriculture on his travels. After spending two years on a farm in Norfolk, he stopped by Flanders to compare animal husbandry techniques with what he learned in England. In 1754, he decided to cultivate farmland in Berwickshire that his father had left for him. For 14 years, Hutton farmed the lands and applied scientific principles to improve his crop yields. While farming, Hutton became captivated with the fate of the soil. Over time the soil was washed away, ending up in streams that eventually channeled into the oceans. He must have wondered why this process did not result in a completely flat Earth over a long period of time. He was successful not only in his farming, but also in a business venture manufacturing ammonium chloride from soot, a process he had helped to work out with a friend. In 1768, with his finances secure, he leased his farmland and moved to Edinburgh, where he could spend more time studying science.

While in Edinburgh, he made many friends among scientific acquaintances, including the chemist Joseph Black, who discovered fixed air (carbon dioxide), and the famous economist Adam Smith. These three founded the Oyster Club, a small society that met weekly to discuss various issues over dinner and to go on field trips together. The affable environment afforded frequent scholarly discussions, and Hutton read voraciously on all matters of science. Enjoyable promenades opened his eyes to the idea that the lands on which he walked were not as they had always been. He also joined a society that became the Royal Society of Edinburgh in 1783. A deepening interest in geology sent him all over Scotland, England, and Wales to pore over the rocks, strata, and landscapes, searching for clues to the Earth's history. He made observations and collected data, formulating a theory that changed the course of geological science.

"Theory of the Earth"

On March 7, 1785, Hutton was to read his paper titled, "Theory of the Earth; or an Investigation of the Laws Observable in the

Composition, Dissolution, and Restoration of Land Upon the Globe," to the newly chartered Royal Society of Edinburgh. However, he became overly nervous from the anticipation and the task fell to his friend, Joseph Black. He had recovered by the next meeting on April 4, when he read the remainder of his paper.

At the time, the prevailing theory for the Earth's formation emphasized the importance of water. German geologist Abraham Gottlob Werner piloted this group of *neptunists*, who believed that the Earth's surface was formed by sedimentary deposition in a great turbulent ocean. Of course, many believed this great ocean was the result of a giant flood as described in the biblical book of Genesis. Literal interpretation of the Bible led many to accept the age of the Earth as approximately 6,000 years old. Hutton did not think this corresponded with the evidence he observed.

In a stroke of genius, Hutton resolved that the history of the Earth must be explained by events of the present. In other words, the natural processes that are observed today were the same processes that sculpted the Earth's surface into its current form. He thought the Earth was constantly but slowly changing and that the changes still were occurring. Events such as volcanic eruptions, *weathering*, and erosion must have had tremendous effects over long periods of time. Hutton was a deist, meaning he believed that nature itself provided evidence of wisdom and design, but after creation, God did not assume control over it. Because Hutton did not believe in a literal interpretation of the Bible, his thinking was not confined to a 6,000-year time frame. In fact, such a short time frame would not allow for the completion of the indeterminate number of cycles, the occurrence of which he had seen evidence. He imagined a much older Earth and postulated that the natural shaping processes of degradation and upheaval were timeless.

This offended many scientists, but Hutton was not just randomly brainstorming or trying to stir up controversy. He based his conclusions on years of careful observation, from which his theory logically germinated. After formulating a hypothesis, Hutton tried to predict what would be observed if the hypothesis were true. Then he roamed the land in search of evidence.

The Effect of Natural Processes on the Shape of the Earth

Hutton noticed that rocks consisted of strata, parallel orderly layers of consolidated sediment. The layers were composed of different materials that must have been derived from rocks even older than themselves. He thought this was similar to what was currently happening on the ocean floor, where a new layer of sediment was forming. This new layer of sediment contained bits and pieces of material that had been worn away from the land of some preexisting *continent* and carried out to sea by the natural flowing of waters. Hutton believed the subterranean heat emanating from the interior of the Earth transformed these layers into solid structures. He was aware of the roles that pressure also played: the compaction from upper layers and the prevention of volatile substances from escaping. Thus the layers of sediment became consolidated after being compacted and cooked for long periods of time.

How could this mechanism account for the formation of mountains? If strata were formed under the sea, what about landmasses that existed thousands of feet above sea level? Hutton again believed that some power underneath the surface of the Earth was responsible. He witnessed powerful volcanic eruptions that he thought were the result of great expansion of the burning *igneous* matter in the interior of the Earth. He proposed that these great expansions also occurred in the geological past. They caused convulsions that ripped up through the ground and forced rock and crust upward, causing bending and folding, forming mountains and hills. *Magma* that had not penetrated the Earth's surface during volcanic activity cooled and solidified, forming granite or other crystalline rocks. This in itself was a novel proposition, since at the time, the existence of igneous rocks as a type of rock completely separate from sedimentary rock was not recognized. If this were all true, then he predicted that arrangements should exist in the strata such that some upturned strata would be vertical or tilted relative to undisturbed layers. One would expect the slanted strata to have been eroded, and then eventually be overlaid by a new layer of horizontal sedimentary rock. Such structures, called *unconformities*, are

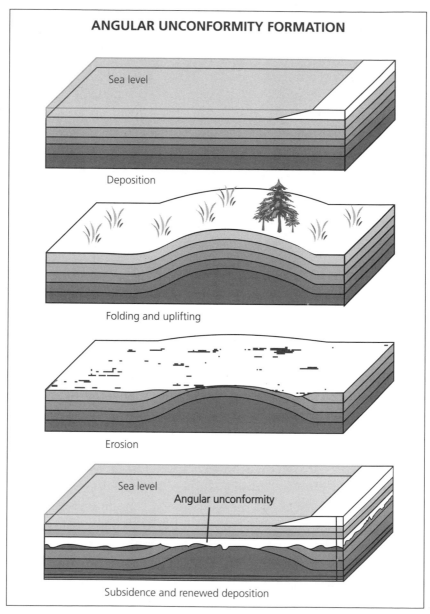

ANGULAR UNCONFORMITY FORMATION

Sea level

Deposition

Folding and uplifting

Erosion

Sea level

Angular unconformity

Subsidence and renewed deposition

An angular unconformity forms when an underlying, eroded, tilted strata is overlaid by horizontal layers.

quite prevalent. One famous locale, called Hutton's Unconformity, is located near his home in Berwickshire, along the west coast at Siccar Point.

Erosion played a key role in Hutton's theory of how the Earth was sculpted. Dry land decayed unremittingly. Flowing water and pounding waves ate away at rock beds. Wind and weathering acted upon exposed surfaces of mountains, producing new soils. Glaciers broke loose and transported chunks of rocky matter with them. Loose soil containing mineral components and organic matter was washed away by rain, and silt was carried by rivers. Chemical reactions in water caused particulate matter to precipitate out of solution. Eventually, all of the loose particulate matter made its way to the oceans, where the sediment settled and was compacted to form a new layer of strata, completing the geological cycle.

Hutton was the first to recognize that igneous rocks were younger than the rocks in which they were found. Sometimes veins of

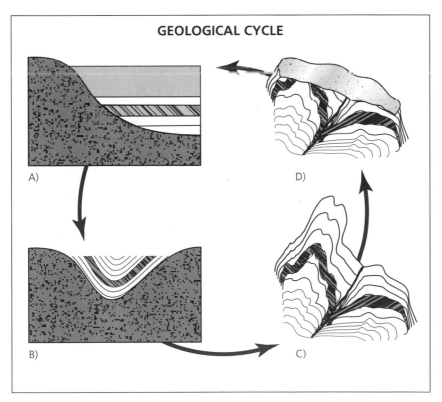

GEOLOGICAL CYCLE

A)

B)

C)

D)

Hutton proposed the Earth was formed by a repeated cycle of geological events, including A) sedimentation, B) burial in the crust, C) mountain building, and D) erosion.

unstratified rock were observed. Hutton had predicted these would occur if the granite in these veins was once melted, and that during the forceful convulsions it was pushed up and outward into cracks that resulted from the violent tremors. The problem with this idea was that no one understood the origin or composition of granite.

Opposition

The neptunists repudiated everything Hutton claimed. They argued that melted rocks cooled into glassy rather than crystalline forms. However, substances that precipitated out of aqueous solutions would form crystals. The action of intense heat on stones such as *limestone* would cause decomposition before being allowed to cool. Regarding the formation of mountains, neptunists also proposed that sedimentary layers were formed underwater but that the ocean was formerly much deeper. Sometimes particulate matter was deposited in a vertical manner, forming peaks under the water. Then the water subsided, the neptunists said, leaving peaks behind as the water level decreased. Neptunists explained veins of unstratified rocks as cracks into which aqueous material containing mineral deposits trickled down. The material hardened over time and left behind the observed intrusions.

When Hutton first presented his ideas, he also published an awkwardly written, anonymous, 30-page pamphlet, *Abstract of a Dissertation . . . Concerning the System of the Earth, Its Duration, and Stability*, summarizing his conclusions. As monumental as Hutton's notions were, they seemed to go largely unnoticed. Those who did notice found them complicated. Opposition not only occurred from neptunists, but also from *catastrophists*, who believed that periodic Earth-shattering events, not slow-working incessant forces, were responsible for creating geological structures. Three years after his initial presentation in Edinburgh, "Theory of the Earth . . ." was published in the first volume of *Transactions of the Royal Society of Edinburgh* (1788).

Irish chemist Richard Kirwan published an attack on Hutton's theory in 1793. Kirwan was the president of the Royal Irish Academy and a staunch Werner devotee. Kirwan attacked Hutton's works from religious and scientific standpoints. Scientifically he refuted the significance of erosion, the importance of heat in consolidation of sediment, and the idea that granite could crystallize from a melt. Hutton was angered and felt his ideas were misrepresented in Kirwan's account.

This printed assault induced Hutton finally to write a full account of his theory for the formation of the Earth with fuller explanations than he had included in the paper published by the Royal Society. In 1795, Hutton published a 1,204-page, two-volume text, *Theory of the Earth with Proofs and Illustrations.* A 267-page third volume was found and published by the Geological Society in 1899, over 100 years after Hutton's death.

After 1791, Hutton was frequently ill with a kidney and bladder ailment. He died on March 26, 1797. He was in the process of preparing an agricultural volume. He had amassed a respectable rock collection, which was donated by one of his sisters to the Royal Society of Edinburgh and then later passed to the university museum. Unfortunately, the collection has since been lost. Though he devoted himself to geological studies, Hutton was widely read and well-versed in a variety of subjects. He had published works on agriculture, meteorology, chemistry, the theory of matter, moral philosophy, and metaphysics.

James Hutton was a sociable, cheerful man with a winning personality. Though he never married, he had many close friends and staunch supporters. He had one illegitimate son, named James, born around 1747, with whom he remained in contact throughout his life. His activities were not limited to promoting his own interests, and he volunteered his talents to a variety of causes. He was an active member on a committee involved in managing a project to join the Fourth and Clyde Rivers with a canal. In 1788, he was elected a foreign member of the French Royal Society of Agriculture.

In 1802, one of Hutton's loyal contemporaries, John Playfair, wrote a biography of James Hutton titled *Illustrations of the Huttonian Theory.* In it, he not only discussed the life of the now famous geologist, but also explained Hutton's theory much more clearly than Hutton himself had. Thirty years later, when society was better prepared to accept the notion that the world was more than 6,000 years old and that it was continually evolving, Playfair's interpretation helped the scientific community adopt Hutton's vision.

Support for Hutton's Theory

After Hutton's death, Scottish geologist and chemist James Hall published evidence supporting his friend's theory. Hall initially had rejected Hutton's theory, but over time and after numerous discussions and tours around Britain with Hutton, he became convinced of the truth of the geological cycle. Hall tried to persuade Hutton to perform certain experiments that would support his claims, but Hutton did not deem them necessary. Hutton felt the principles he delineated were clearly evident by observing nature and that nothing in a laboratory could significantly replicate the power of nature. Out of respect for Hutton, Hall refrained from pushing the issue. But after his death, Hall published several experiments that challenged the objections to Hutton's ideas, bringing Hutton's theory into the limelight.

Hall's first experiment demonstrated that igneous rocks could be converted to crystalline rocks. Neptunists did not believe that igneous

Today Hutton's ideas are summarized in the principle of uniformitarianism, which holds that the physical and chemical processes that occur today are the same as those that formed geological structures in the past, though it may be on an altered timescale. Uniformitarianism may be summarized as "the present is the key to the past," a tenet that forms the basis of modern geology.

CHRONOLOGY

1726	James Hutton is born on June 3, in Edinburgh, Scotland
1740	Enters Edinburgh University to study humanities and becomes interested in chemistry
1743	Begins a law apprenticeship
1744–47	Studies medicine at the University of Edinburgh

rocks were once liquid but thought that if they were, they should turn into glass upon cooling, not crystalline rocks. By slowing down the cooling process, Hall was able to form an opaque crystalline material after melting fused basalt. Some were impressed by this. Others thought the results were sketchy, that perhaps some component was lost during the reaction that changed the chemical composition of the material. Next, Hall attacked the idea that marble could not be produced from limestone. It was thought that carbon dioxide would escape as a gas and only quicklime would result. So Hall heated limestone (a powdered chalk) in a sealed gun barrel to allow immense pressure to build up. This prevented the escape of any volatile components during the heating. Then he slowly cooled it and to his delight found marble inside! In another experiment, Hall was able to produce consolidated *sandstone* from heating sand with salt water. Incidentally, the series of over 500 experiments Hall performed in his quest to validate Hutton's claims earned himself the title of founder of experimental geology and geochemistry.

1747	Moves to Paris to study anatomy
1749	Moves to Leiden, receives a medical degree, and enters a business venture making sal ammoniac
1750	Returns to Edinburgh and develops an interest in geology and mineralogy
1754–68	Farms in Berwickshire
1768	Returns to Edinburgh to pursue geological studies
1785	Hutton presents his paper, "Theory of the Earth," to the Royal Society of Edinburgh
1788	Publishes "Theory of the Earth" in *Transactions of the Royal Society of Edinburgh*
1795	Publishes *Theory of the Earth with Proofs and Illustrations* in two volumes

1797	Dies on March 26 in Edinburgh
1899	The third volume of *Theory of the Earth* is published posthumously

FURTHER READING

Carruthers, Margaret W., and Susan Clinton. *Pioneers of Geology: Discovering Earth's Secrets.* New York: Franklin Watts, 2001. Includes a chapter on Hutton that chronicles his pioneering research in geology.

Electric Scotland. "Significant Scots: James Hutton." Available online. URL: http://www.electricscotland.com/history/other/hutton_james.htm. Accessed January 15, 2005. Has information on Scottish clans and profiles of Scottish-born people who have made significant contributions to history.

Gillispie, Charles C., ed. *Dictionary of Scientific Biography.* Vol. 6. New York: Scribner, 1970–76. Good source for facts concerning Hutton's personal background and scientific accomplishments but assumes reader has basic knowledge of science.

Repcheck, Jack. *The Man Who Found Time: James Hutton and the Discovery of the Earth's Antiquity.* Cambridge, Mass.: Perseus, 2003. Traces Hutton's life, ideas, and inspiration that led to the development of the concept of an ancient Earth.

Alexander von Humboldt 4

(1769–1859)

Alexander von Humboldt was a true polymath, or walking encyclopedia. (*Library of Congress, Prints and Photographs Division [LC-USZ62-110637]*)

Unification of the Natural Sciences

Science is often separated into several disciplines that seem related only because they all employ the scientific method. For example, geology is the scientific study of the Earth, its origins and *evolution*, the materials from which it is made, and the processes that act on it. Biology is the science of living beings and life processes. At first glance, the two disciplines may not seem related in scope, but they are. The Earth's structure in a particular location affects life-forms and their lifestyles. Furthermore, life-forms can alter the structure or the physical and chemical composition of their habitat, particularly over long periods of time. A polymathic scientist and explorer named Alexander von Humboldt embraced a philosophy of unification of the natural sciences long before the rest of the scientific world. His aspiration was to discover the connections among all natural phenomena. He explored geographic regions that were practically unknown to the scientific world in search of natural laws that connected landforms, climate, and organisms.

A Career in Politics or Mining

Friedrich Wilhelm Karl Heinrich Alexander von Humboldt was born September 14, 1769, in Berlin, the capital of the kingdom of Prussia. His father, Alexander Georg von Humboldt was an army officer and aristocrat. His mother was Maria Elizabeth von Hollwege, a wealthy but stoic woman. As a child, Alexander was often sick and confined to his home. He especially appreciated the time he spent with his father strolling around and exploring nature at the family's countryside estate in Bradenburg, Schloss Tegel. Alexander's father died when he was only 10, leaving his mother in charge of his and his older brother Wilhelm's education. The boys were taught mostly by private tutors and studied the classics, history, languages, mathematics, politics, and economics. Their mother hoped they would obtain positions in the government when they grew up, but Alexander enjoyed botany and natural history and preferred to spend his free time collecting rocks and bugs, which he brought home to study and sketch.

Alexander's mother enrolled him at the University of Frankfurt an der Oder in 1787 to prepare him for a government career. In 1789, he enrolled at the University of Göttingen to study law, but he became even more interested in subjects such as geology, mineralogy, and mining. One of his professors introduced him to Georg Forster, a scholar and explorer who had accompanied the famous captain James Cook on a Pacific Ocean voyage. In 1790, Forster brought Humboldt on a European tour down the Rhine and introduced him to many influential scientists. Forster's tales of travel fascinated Humboldt, who pledged to have his own adventures someday.

Following his mother's wishes, Humboldt enrolled in the Hamburg School of Commerce to study economics, business, and politics. However, a career in politics was his mother's desire, not his. To obtain the training necessary to embark on a scientific career, Humboldt entered the Mining Academy at Freiberg in southern Germany in 1791. The curriculum was both physically and mentally rigorous. The students labored in the mines all morning and studied geology and mineralogy in the afternoons. After successfully completing his studies, Humboldt was offered the enviable position of inspector of the mines in 1792. In this position, he established the first mine laborer training school, a project that he financed from his own pocket. In southern Prussia he actively participated in mine inspections. He also collected plant specimens and mineral samples from deep within the mine shafts and tunnels. From these botanical pursuits, he wrote his first scientific piece on plant physiology, but he did not ignore his obligations to Prussia's mining department. His efforts miraculously increased by six-fold the mineral output of mines thought to be depleted. As a result, he was offered a promotion, which he declined. He was making other plans.

An Exotic Expedition

Humboldt's mother died of breast cancer in November 1796, leaving him a large fortune. Without hesitation, he quit his mining position and started planning his own scientific expedition. The Napoleonic Wars made travel difficult, so his plans were continually delayed. In 1799 Humboldt met up with Aimé Bonpland, a French physician and botanist. Humboldt's reputation for mining successes led to a break from King Charles IV of Spain. The king sanctioned safe passage and exploration of Spain's Central and South American colonies, hoping that Humboldt would find gold and diamonds as he did in Prussia. Humboldt was granted access to exotic countries such as Cuba, Mexico, Venezuela, Colombia, Ecuador, Peru, Chile, Argentina, and the Philippines, which had been closed to Europeans for three centuries.

Humboldt and Bonpland spent a few months preparing and gathering all the necessary supplies, instruments, notebooks, equipment, and crew. They departed from La Coruña, Spain, on June 5, 1799. Humboldt wasted no time during the oceanic voyage. He immediately began collecting data on marine life and seawater chemistry and measuring air and ocean temperatures and the Sun's position. When typhoid fever broke out on the ship, instead of arriving in Havana, Cuba, the crew was forced to land at Cumaná, Venezuela, in early July.

Though the typhoid epidemic was unfortunate, landing at Cumaná was exhilarating for the two young explorers. From the moment they stepped off the ship they were thrilled at the abundant display of new tropical life. After spending three months attempting to classify all the unfamiliar flora and fauna, they finally penetrated the rain forest on the backs of mules. Again they were amazed at the greenness and the richness of the life that surrounded them. They collected as many biological specimens as they could pack on their mules. As Humboldt directed his energies toward the rocks and minerals of the region, he was relieved to find them similar to those in Europe. Damage from earthquakes gave evidence to the violent subterranean forces at work shaping the Earth, and Humboldt began to ponder the geological relationship between the continents.

In November 1799, Humboldt and Bonpland sailed for Caracas, the capital of Venezuela. On the way they witnessed an enormous meteor shower. In Caracas, they rented a house for the duration of the rainy season and tried to organize the multitude of specimens that they had already gathered. They catalogued them and wrote letters home detailing their explorations to this point. So far they had collected more than 1,600 plant specimens.

Rumors of Casiquiare, a natural canal that supposedly connected the Orinoco and the Amazon River basins, caught Humboldt's interest. He wondered if it really existed. If so, it would be the only natural canal to do so. Local Indians and missionaries confirmed the tales and pointed Humboldt in the right direction. He wanted to chart the canal, so in February 1800, Humboldt and Bonpland left the capital city and crossed the coastal mountain range, called the Cordillera. On the way, Humboldt noted the garnet crystals embedded within the mountain rocks. Then they had to cross the llanos, tropical grasslands full of crocodiles, snakes, and cattle herds. This was not a leisurely tourist route but a physically demanding, tiring path.

While traveling, they stopped at the ranching station of Calabozo, where Humboldt was fascinated by electric eels. He wanted to examine one closely but could not get hold of one without being shocked himself. Humboldt accidentally stepped on an eel and suffered fierce pain in his knees and joints for the remainder of the day. To help him out, the local Indians corralled a bunch of horses and mules into a swamp full of the eels. The poor animals were repeatedly stung until the eels ran out of juice. Then he could easily capture one for rigorous analysis.

By the end of March 1800, they had traveled 108 miles (174 km) and reached the end of the llanos. In San Fernando, on the banks of one of the Orinoco's tributaries, the Apure River, they were joined by a Spaniard named Nicholás Soto. The abundant wildlife continued to amaze the explorers. Flamingos, crocodiles, spoonbills, monkeys, jaguars, and capybaras (rodents the size of large dogs) greeted them along the riverside. Based on information they obtained from the locals, they headed onward to Orinoco with a group of hired canoe rowers. En route, Humboldt analyzed the waters and noted geological landmarks. Along the Orinoco they stopped at an island where hundreds of Indians were waiting to harvest turtle eggs from which they could extract oil. Humboldt estimated there were 30 million eggs buried in the sand.

Natives who heard about the European explorers' travel plans warned them against proceeding. They told them tales of one-headed monsters and other atrocities. Despite this, Humboldt exchanged his guides and persisted up the Río Negro. A missionary priest who knew the way accompanied the explorers. They never encountered the foretold monsters, but the mosquitoes were vicious, and the waters were dirty and full of dead animals.

The explorers reached the Casiquiare in the middle of May, finally verifying the rumors of the existence of the natural canal. Humboldt used survey tools to measure and map the exact location of the entrance of the river. The next day, they turned around and began retracing their route. On the way Humboldt visited an ancient burial ground for the *extinct* Atures Indians, from which he took some unauthorized souvenirs, including bones from the graves. In the village of Uruana he noted the use of hallucinogenic plants and the custom of eating dirt. After covering 1,500 miles (2,414 km) on foot and by canoe in search of the Casiquiare, they had to rest for one month in Angostura before crossing the llanos again. Both Humboldt and Bonpland contracted typhoid and needed time to regain their strength. They reached Cumaná again in November 1800, having charted the longitude and latitude of 55 locations.

Humboldt and Bonpland spent the winter touring Cuba and organizing thousands of plant and animal specimens for shipment back to Europe. They also visited the local sugar plantations and tobacco, cotton, and indigo fields, as well as many factories. While he enjoyed the temporary comforts of being in the most developed Spanish colony, Humboldt was appalled at the exploitation of slaves to boost the Cuban economy. He published *Political Essay on the*

Volcanoes

Volcanoes are openings in the Earth's crust from which molten rock and hot gases erupt. They are formed when lava, rock, and hot gases burst forth from the Earth's interior through the surface of the Earth. Below a depth of 15 miles (24 km) or more, the temperature is so hot it literally melts rock, forming magma. As magma is formed, gas is also created. Because it is not as dense as the rock itself, gas-filled magma rises toward the surface of the Earth. It fills magma chambers, pockets of magma located two miles (3.2 km) below the surface that serve as reservoirs. Pressure builds up in the chambers, and the magma melts a channel or conduit in a weakened part of the surrounding rock. Finally, eruption occurs through a vent.

Hot gases, including water vapor, carbon dioxide, sulfur dioxide, and nitrogen, are expelled. So is red hot lava that reaches temperatures of

Island of Cuba (1828), describing the island's geography, landforms, geology, and climate as they related to the island's economy and population.

Humboldt and Bonpland next sailed into Cartagena, Columbia. From there the men hiked 20 miles (32 km) to Turbaco to explore the local gas volcanoes. Then they traveled through the rain forests until they passed the village of Honda, 50 miles (80 km) west of Bogotá. The elevation was approximately 9,000 feet (2,743 m), and Humboldt noticed a change in the vegetation with the increase in altitude. They made it to Bogotá, where they were warmly greeted. Bonpland became feverish, and they ended up staying for two months while he recovered. Humboldt spent time examining the collections of an eminent botanist who resided nearby. He also took several short trips during which he found rock salt, coal fields, and fossilized mastodon bones.

over 2,000°F (1,093°C). Particles of rock called tephra also are ejected. Tephra includes volcanic dust, volcanic ash, and volcanic bombs. Large quantities of volcanic dust affect the climate, as the particles may block sunlight from penetrating the Earth's atmosphere. Volcanic bombs range in diameter from a few inches to several feet.

Volcanoes are most commonly situated over boundaries between the dozen or so tectonic plates of the Earth's outer shell. These plates are enormous slabs of rigid rock that are continuously shifting. The idea of moving plates was proposed by German meteorologist Alfred Wegener in 1912, in a theory called *continental drift*. These motions result in the bumping and separation of adjacent plates, both of which may result in volcanic activity.

If a volcano has erupted recently, it is considered active. Examples of active volcanoes are Mount Saint Helens in the state of Washington and Stromboli off the coast of Italy. If a volcano has not erupted recently it is referred to as dormant. Lassen Peak in California and Kilimanjaro in northern Tanzania are examples of dormant volcanoes. Extinct volcanoes have not erupted recently and are not expected to erupt in the future. Mount Kenya in Kenya is considered extinct.

In September 1801, Humboldt and Bonpland left Bogotá for Quito, Ecuador. They had to travel across the Andes Mountains. The geography was much different than they had experienced in South America thus far. Over the mountains there were cliffs, icy lakes, and peaks and valleys. They passed ancient Inca Empire ruins that intrigued Humboldt, who was interested in anthropology. They climbed a volcano named Puracé and faced obstacles such as mudslides, downpours, and lightning. Once they reached Quito in January 1802, they were surrounded by huge, active, smoky volcanoes. The residents hosted several receptions for the weary travelers and provided them with comfortable living quarters.

Highest Altitude

While in Quito, Humboldt investigated all of the nearby volcanic mountains. He climbed them, examined their geological structures, analyzed their gaseous exhalations and the composition of the surrounding atmosphere, and timed their seismic waves. Mountain climbing was more dangerous back then, as none of the modern sophisticated equipment or techniques were available. Climbers had no special clothing and did not even use ropes. Another difficulty was overcoming mountain sickness, which left people dizzy and nauseous at high altitudes. Nevertheless, Humboldt was fascinated by the volcanoes. Being physically robust, he was determined to climb the Chimborazo, thought to be the highest mountain at the time. The highest known today is Mount Everest, at 29,035 feet (8,850 m). It did not matter to him that no man had ever achieved this or that many never returned at all.

On June 9, 1802, Humboldt set out on a trip to Chimborazo with Bonpland, a young Ecuadorian man named Carlos Montúfar, and several mountain guides. They arrived at the base on June 23 and began their climb. Dangerous cliffs, icy slopes, and clouds that destroyed visibility forced all but one guide to retreat. During the ascent, Humboldt used a tube barometer to calculate their altitude at various positions. Mountain sickness was really taking a toll on the men as they passed 17,000 feet. Not only were they sick and dizzy, but their eyes were bloodshot and their lips and gums were bleeding. Humboldt, who had experienced this on his previous climbs, was not discouraged. They continued upward and were finally rewarded by a spectacular sight never before viewed by human eyes from their record-setting altitude of 19,286 feet (5,878

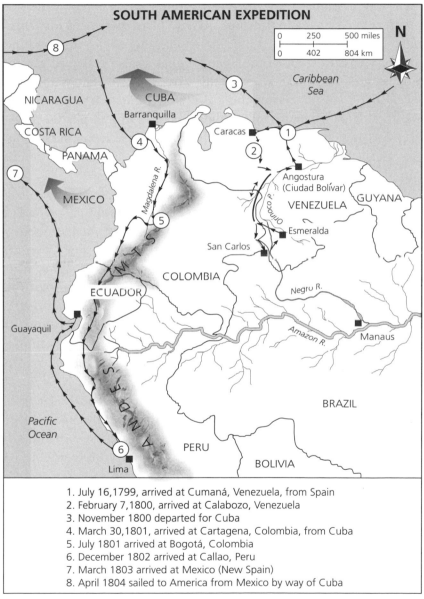

SOUTH AMERICAN EXPEDITION

1. July 16, 1799, arrived at Cumaná, Venezuela, from Spain
2. February 7, 1800, arrived at Calabozo, Venezuela
3. November 1800 departed for Cuba
4. March 30, 1801, arrived at Cartagena, Colombia, from Cuba
5. July 1801 arrived at Bogotá, Colombia
6. December 1802 arrived at Callao, Peru
7. March 1803 arrived at Mexico (New Spain)
8. April 1804 sailed to America from Mexico by way of Cuba

Humboldt first demonstrated his interdisciplinary genius from research he performed during a five-year expedition across South America.

m). Encouraged and exhilarated by their achievement, the men made their way back down, stopping periodically so the tireless Humboldt could chip away rock samples for later examination.

Humboldt and Bonpland, now accompanied by Montúfar, made their way to Lima, Peru, by late October. Again, they needed to organize their data and pack up rock and plant specimens for transport back to Europe. While in Lima, they enjoyed watching Mercury pass in front of the Sun. Humboldt also collected guano, a substance that is made primarily from bird droppings that the locals used as fertilizer. Humboldt shipped some back to Europe for chemical analysis, and it was found to be rich in phosphates. A few decades later, tons of guano were exported to Europe, increasing European food production and improving the economy of South America.

On Christmas Eve, the trio departed from Callao, Peru, on a ship for Guayaquil, Ecuador. During this trip Humboldt studied the cold currents to the west of Peru. Today this phenomenon is called the Peru Current, also known as the Humboldt Current, and it has a significant impact on the regional economy. They next departed for Acapulco, Mexico. As they left the port, one of the volcanoes Humboldt had climbed while in Quito, the Cotopaxi, erupted, causing booming sound effects. In Mexico, Humboldt mapped the exact location of Acapulco, which was positioned incorrectly on the current maps. He also toured the Guerrero Mountains on mule and horseback and observed the geological *outcrops*. He recorded the longitude and latitude of several significant landmarks and spent a lot of time in the government archives in Mexico City. While visiting the mountain region, Guanjuato, Humboldt explored the silver mines and collected mineral specimens. A special mule train was required to transport the numerous specimens. He visited the location of a volcano formed only 44 years before, named Jorullo. The lava fields were still smoldering, and Humboldt measured gases and shocked the Indians by climbing into the crater itself.

Humboldt, Bonpland, and Montúfar left Mexico in January 1804 and went to Washington, D.C., where their reputation preceded them. Everyone wanted to meet the men who had climbed Chimborazo and lived to tell about it. Humboldt was anxious to meet President Thomas Jefferson. As president of the American Philosophical Society, Jefferson was well aware of Humboldt's scientific exploits as well as his fame as an adventurous explorer. The two men formed a strong friendship and corresponded for the rest of their lives. The impression Humboldt left on Americans before sailing home is evidenced by the numerous cities, mountains, bays, and parks named after him.

The Larger Task That Lay Ahead

The party arrived in France in August 1804. To Humboldt's amusement, he learned that the French thought he had died of yellow fever during his travels. The rumors increased his fame even more. It is reported that during his lifetime, he was second in fame only to Napoleon, who incidentally, was jealous of Humboldt's popularity and publicly belittled him by comparing him to his wife, calling them both "flower collectors."

Though the American expedition was over, Humboldt's greater task of communicating all he had learned and observed lay ahead of him. He took trips to Italy and Berlin but settled in Paris, where he was surrounded by other scientists, libraries, publishers, and engravers, to begin writing his manuscripts. The vast amounts of information he gathered placed Humboldt in a position no previous scientist had occupied. He was a true polymath, an expert on everything, a walking encyclopedia of knowledge. He amassed huge amounts of data on magnetism, geology, meteorology, climatology, geography, mineralogy, zoology, botany, astronomy, anthropology, and more. Humboldt and Bonpland collected over 60,000 plant specimens, 10 percent of which were unknown in Europe. In addition, from his research, the new field of plant geography was founded. Plant geography is concerned with how climate and the history of the planet affect the locations of plant populations. In particular, from his observations of plants occurring at different altitudes along mountains, Humboldt concluded that the populations of plants could be predicted given the climate and altitude.

Humboldt started his scientific career as a neptunist, that is, a follower of Abraham Gottlob Werner. Werner taught mineralogy

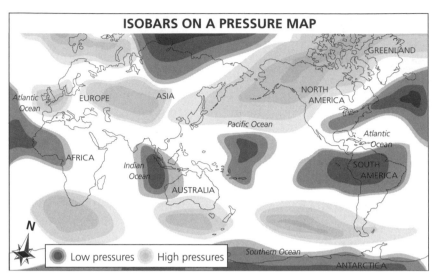

ISOBARS ON A PRESSURE MAP

Humboldt was the first to use isotherms and isobars, an example of which is shown here.

at Freiberg and was the leader of the neptunists, who believed that all rock was formed from sediment or precipitate of a universal ocean. Werner also believed and taught that *basalt* was of an aqueous origin. Empirical studies, in particular those of the volcanoes surrounding Quito, convinced Humboldt that basalt was of an igneous origin. He believed that volcanic activity was responsible for shaping the Earth. He also correlated the linear pattern of volcanoes to underground fissures and looked for correlations between geological structures and geographical elements.

With respect to the Earth's magnetism, Humboldt found that the intensity declined as one moved from the poles toward the equator. In Paris, Humboldt met with French chemist Joseph Gay-Lussac to study the law of magnetic declination. He returned to research on geomagnetism later in his life.

Investigations on climate and meteorology also filled many of Humboldt's notebooks. He found there was an overall decrease in temperature with an increase in altitude and was the first person to chart *isotherms* and *isobars*. Isotherms are plots on a map which connect areas that have the same mean temperature. Isobars are lines on a map that connect points with equal air pressure.

Humboldt estimated that it would take five or six years to complete approximately 17 volumes about his South American field studies. In the end, it took him 30 years and 30 volumes. The series was titled *Voyages to the Equinoctial Regions of the New Continent Made During the Years 1799 to 1804* (1807–39). The volumes covered topics such as plant geography, astronomy, botany, and even social and political essays. In addition to the many scientific volumes, Humboldt also wrote separate volumes intended for the general public. Remarkably, this series included 1,400 illustrations, which cost more to publish than the expedition itself and resulted in the depletion of the remainder of the fortune from his mother's inheritance. In need of a regular income, Humboldt accepted a position as a court chancellor and moved back to Berlin in 1827.

Diamonds in the Urals

Russia's finance minister requested Humboldt's expertise soon after his return to Berlin. Humboldt was invited to explore the Ural Mountains at the czar's expense in the hope of finding valuable mineral deposits. Even though he was 59, Humboldt was thrilled at the opportunity to explore this virtually unknown territory. He was anxious to explore the Earth's magnetism using Russia as his field laboratory. He recruited a biologist and physician named Christian Gottfried Ehrenberg, a chemist and mineralogist named Gustav Rose, and his own valet, Karl Seifert, to accompany him. They set out by horse and carriage on April 12, 1829.

The men traveled through eastern Europe, St. Petersburg, Moscow, and on to the Urals. Every so often Humboldt measured and recorded the magnetic intensity of the earth and took astronomical observations. There were no inns en route, so they slept in the carriages on the frozen Siberian plains. On June 15, they reached Ekaterinburg, a town in the central Urals that they used as a base. Already they had 14 boxes of mostly rock and mineral specimens to ship back to St. Petersburg and Berlin. From this town they hiked to the mines and studied mineral deposits. They examined specimens of iron, copper, gold, and platinum as well as

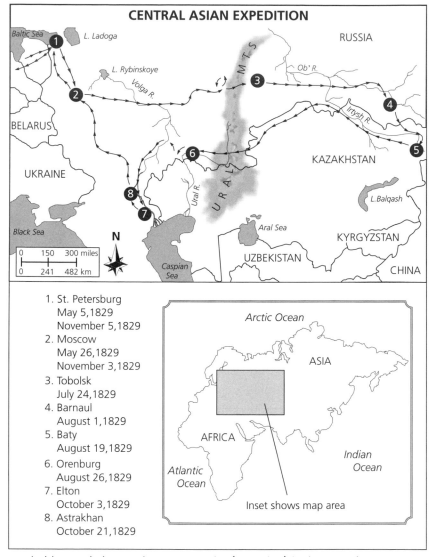

CENTRAL ASIAN EXPEDITION

1. St. Petersburg
   May 5,1829
   November 5,1829
2. Moscow
   May 26,1829
   November 3,1829
3. Tobolsk
   July 24,1829
4. Barnaul
   August 1,1829
5. Baty
   August 19,1829
6. Orenburg
   August 26,1829
7. Elton
   October 3,1829
8. Astrakhan
   October 21,1829

Inset shows map area

Humboldt traveled more than 12,000 miles (19,312 km) by horse and carriage across Central Asia.

others. Humboldt learned during his previous travels that diamonds were often found where gold and platinum were located. Soon after he suggested they search the area, diamonds were successfully located. As a result, Humboldt was credited with discovering Russia's first diamond field.

After exploring the Urals, the men continued across the hot, mosquito-infested, grassy steppes of Siberia until they reached the Russian border with China. Then they turned around. By the time they arrived at Moscow in November 1829, they had traveled 12,000 miles (19,312 km). Rose published some mineralogical and

Geomagnetism

Geomagnetism refers to the magnetism of the Earth. The Earth acts like a giant spherical magnet with a magnetic north and south pole that create a magnetic field. This is the basis for the functioning of simple magnets. The magnetized needle of a simple compass aligns itself with the Earth's magnetic field so that it points toward the North Pole. The intensity of the magnetic field is strongest at the poles and weakest at the equator.

The geographic North Pole is not exactly the same as the magnetic north pole. The angle between the magnetic and geographic North Pole is called the magnetic declination, which varies by location. This was of particular interest to Humboldt, who measured the tilt of the magnetic field from the Earth's axis of rotation to be approximately seven degrees.

The geomagnetic field is generated by the motion of electric charges in the liquid outer core that lies under the Earth's crust and *mantle*. The magnetic field of the Earth changes over time. In the history of the Earth, the field has completely reversed direction several times. Ancient rocks formed from cooling lava provide preserved evidence about the Earth's magnetic field at the time when the rock was formed. By studying differences in the Earth's magnetic fields over time, geologists can also learn about the history of the drifting of the continents.

geological findings, and Humboldt published three volumes of *Central Asia* in 1843. The first two volumes described the Asian mountain ranges, and the third covered magnetic and climatological observations. Significantly, Humboldt was able to convince the Russian government to establish several magnetic and meteorological observation stations. Eventually, the British did also. This effort was the first major international scientific collaboration. From information gathered at these stations, Humboldt developed the principle of continentality, which describes the moderating effect of proximity to large water bodies on regional climate.

Cosmic Comprehension

A few years later, Humboldt began composing his magnum opus, *Cosmos*, an attempt to describe the workings of the entire universe for the general public. Published in five mammoth volumes (1845–62), it included scientific descriptions of the physical Earth and also descriptions of the heavens and of all life. Humboldt explained the interdependence of the natural sciences, a principle that pervades modern sciences but was novel at the time. Geology affects climate. Climate affects life-forms. Life-forms affect the environment and leave imprints on nascent rock-forms, and so on. This was also the beginning of ecology, the study of the relationships between organisms and their environments.

Alexander von Humboldt was not able to complete the *Cosmos* series. He died at age 89, on May 6, 1859. He was given a state funeral and buried at Schloss Tegel, his family's countryside estate. He bequeathed his estate to his devoted servant, Seifert. Called the most learned man of his time, Humboldt was awarded several honorary doctorate degrees and elected to membership in all of the prestigious academic organizations. The Royal Society of London awarded him the Copley Medal in 1852.

Humboldt's work instigated advancements in several fields in the Earth sciences such as oceanography and geomagnetism. Plant geography helped stimulate British biologist Alfred Wallace to develop the theory of evolution, and Humboldt's South American travels inspired British biologist Charles Darwin to do the same. Humboldt's observations on the complementary jigsaw puzzle piece pattern of the South American east coast and the African west coast influenced Alfred Wegener's proposal of the continental drift theory. Humboldt was skilled at recognizing the economic benefits of local biological and geological features such as diamonds, guano, and the Peru Current, thus his studies affected politics and economics as well as science. No doubt this pleased Humboldt, as he was a man for whom no boundaries existed between disciplines. He was a pioneer in the Earth sciences not only for the enormous amount of data he collected during his explorations, but also for unifying physical geography, geology, climatology, and biology. Only a man who wholly understood nature could describe nature as a whole.

CHRONOLOGY

1769	Alexander von Humboldt is born on September 12 in Berlin, Germany
1787	Enrolls at the University of Frankfurt an der Oder
1789	Enters the University of Göttingen with plans to study law but becomes interested in science
1790	Tours Europe with the explorer Georg Forster
1791	Enters Mining Academy at Freiberg
1792–97	Gains employment with Prussia's mining department and establishes the first mine laborer training school
1799–1804	Travels to the Americas with Aimé Bonpland, studies Venezuela's grasslands, maps the course of the Orinoco River, verifies the existence of the Casiquiare Canal, studies volcanic mountains, and observes different life-forms at different altitudes
1804	Returns to Europe and begins compiling data and writing observations from his expedition
1807–39	Publishes *Voyages to the Equinoctial Regions of the New Continent Made During the Years 1799 to 1804* in 30 volumes
1827	Accepts position as court chancellor in Berlin

1828	Publishes *Political Essay on the Island of Cuba*
1829	Explores the geography, geology, and climate of the Russian Empire
1843	Publishes *Central Asia,* a three-volume report of geographic, geological, and climatological observations
1845–62	*Cosmos* is published in five volumes
1859	Dies in Berlin on May 6

FURTHER READING

Allaby, Michael, and Derek Gjertsen, eds. *Makers of Science.* Vol. 2. New York: Oxford University Press, 2002. Describes the achievements of the world's most famous scientists within their historical contexts. Attractive illustrations.

De Terra, Helmut. *Humboldt: The Life and Times of Alexander von Humboldt, 1769–1859.* New York: Alfred A. Knopf, 1955. Extensive, authoritative biography describing Humboldt's strengths and weaknesses and his contributions as a scientist and an explorer. Intended for advanced readers.

Gaines, Ann. *Alexander von Humboldt: Colossus of Exploration.* New York: Chelsea House, 1997. Thorough accounting of Humboldt's travel itineraries, with minimal explanations of scientific discoveries. Appropriate for young adult readers.

Gillispie, Charles C., ed. *Dictionary of Scientific Biography.* Vol. 6. New York: Scribner, 1970–76. Good source for facts concerning personal backgrounds and scientific accomplishments but assumes reader his basic knowledge of science.

Meadows, Jack. *The Great Scientists: The Story of Science Told Through the Lives of Twelve Landmark Figures.* New York: Oxford University Press, 1987. Brief biographies of 12 high-profile scientists and the development of science as influenced by social forces. Colorful illustrations.

Georges Cuvier

(1769–1832)

Georges Cuvier is considered the
father of vertebrate paleontology.
*(George Bernard/Science Photo
Library/Photo Researchers, Inc.)*

The Reality of Extinction of Past Life-forms

The word *extinct* often calls to mind ancient animals such as
dinosaurs or dodo birds. It might remind some people of animals
currently on the endangered species list. Two centuries ago, the
concept that animals can become extinct was not widely accepted.
People could not believe that animals never seen by human eyes
had once crawled, walked, and hopped over Earth's surface.

Georges Cuvier demonstrated that unknown animals really did exist and were gone forever. He suggested that catastrophic events had annihilated ancient species. Though he earned his reputation as a brilliant paleontologist, someone who studies fossils, he was actually trained as a biologist. He used his knowledge of comparative anatomy of *extant* (still living) and extinct creatures to learn about the history of the Earth.

Birth in Montbéliard

Georges Cuvier was born on August 23, 1769, in Montbéliard. At the time, Montbéliard was under the jurisdiction of the German duke of Württemberg, but it was a French-speaking community. In 1793, the territory was annexed by France, and Cuvier became a French citizen. He was baptized as Jean-Léopold-Nicolas-Frédéric Cuvier. Later his mother added Dagobert (name of an ancient French king) to his name. When his elder brother, Georges, died as a child, he adopted the name Georges and used it for the rest of his life. As a child, Georges spent time sketching various animals he read about in a 44-volume encyclopedia about the natural world, *Natural History*, written by Georges-Louis Leclerc, comte de Buffon. Georges was a skilled artist and later in life provided many of the drawings for his own published works.

Though his parents wanted him to go into the ministry, Georges's teachers did not recommend him for a scholarship to theology school. Georges's father was a soldier, and the family did not have enough money to send him. Fortunately, Georges gained admittance to Caroline University, in Stuttgart, Germany, a school founded by the duke of Württemberg. From 1784 to 1788, he studied a variety of subjects ranging from administration and economics to the scientific discipline of zoology and the art of dissection. Georges also mastered the German language.

A Man with Many Titles

After graduation Georges's father helped him obtain a position as a private tutor for an aristocratic family in Normandy, France. This protected him from the immediate effects of the French Revolution and allowed him to indulge in independent studies of natural history during his free time. He collected fish, mollusk, and shorebird specimens from the nearby port of Fécamp and kept detailed notes of his dissections, observations, and sketches in scientific diaries. During this time, Cuvier regularly corresponded with a friend from Caroline University, Christian Heinrich Pfaff. These letters, which mentioned many of the scientific ideas for which Cuvier became famous in the early 1800s, were probably circulated among other budding German scientists. In them, he described his scientific endeavors and wrote about topics such as the geology of Normandy and the bands of flint nodules within the chalk beds. Cuvier and his notebooks came to the attention of French naturalists, and they encouraged him to come to Paris.

In 1795, he found himself teaching animal anatomy at the recently reformed Musée National d'Histoire Naturelle (National Museum of Natural History), the largest institution dedicated to scientific research at the time. Having a proper forum, he promptly presented the results of his Normandy research. Cuvier was a gifted teacher and was soon given the position professor of zoology at the Écoles Centrales. His abilities and reputation led to several other responsibilities and appointments. In 1796, he became the youngest member of the Class of Physical Sciences at the Institut de France (Institute of France, hereafter referred to as the Institute), which partly replaced the Royal Academy of Sciences. In 1800, he was appointed professor at the Collège de France, and he was appointed professor of comparative anatomy at the Musée in 1802. He became permanent secretary of the physical sciences for the Institute in 1803. Napoleon appointed him university counselor in 1808 and sent him to reorganize higher education in Italy, the Netherlands, and southern Germany. As compensation, Cuvier received the title of chevalier in 1811, awarding him the privileges of a low-ranking nobleman. In 1814, Cuvier became councillor of state and head of the Interior Department of the Council of State from 1819 until his death. Cuvier was elected a member of the Académie française in 1818. He was made a baron in 1819 and a grand officier of the Legion of Honor in 1824. In 1831, Cuvier was nominated a peer of France, an honor of high-ranking noblemen.

Identification of Animals from Fossil Remains

In 1796, Cuvier presented to the Institute his treatise *Memoir on the Species of Elephants, Both Living and Fossils.* He gave a detailed description of the *osteological* (related to the study of bones) features of two known elephant species, African and Indian. He discussed their teeth, skulls, and jaws, among other structures. Then he confidently claimed that fossil elephant remains belonged to a distinct third species, identified as *Elephas primigenius,* an extinct, hairy mammoth. Cuvier also suggested that comparative anatomy could be used to learn about geological history. For example, one popular geological theory was that the Earth had been gradually cooling since its formation. Scientists assumed that locations where elephant remains were found must have previously been warmer.

Fossils and Paleontology

Though long ago the term *fossil* meant anything that came from the ground, today it is reserved for the remains or traces of a formerly living organism. Ancient bones and animal tracks found in sediment are both considered fossils. The word fossil is also used to refer to combustible fuels that are biological in origin (such as coal or natural gas). Fossils from aquatic life are more common than terrestrial life, as deposition of loose sediment washed away by erosion occurs in bodies of water. Normally the remains of dead organisms are decomposed by microorganisms but sometimes the remains are preserved. Hard materials such as bones and teeth can be found essentially unaltered. Even softer parts might be found intact if the organism was quickly frozen in a block of ice. Other fossil remains become petrified, meaning that minerals have replaced the organic matter and hardened. This process usually preserves the basic

Cuvier responded that since the remains belonged to an entirely new species, the extinct animal might have been better adapted to cooler climates than the living species, thus the Earth might not necessarily be cooling. Nevertheless, Cuvier claimed there must have been a primitive, prehuman world that was destroyed by some major catastrophe. He wisely left the determination of the specific nature of the cataclysmic event to experts in geology.

Later that year Cuvier was sent plates of fossil bones found in South America. Using careful anatomical comparison, he concluded that this elephant-sized beast that he named megatherium was also extinct. He concluded that it was another animal from the ancient world. These studies increased Cuvier's interest in fossil anatomy and set him on a mission to study all fossil animals.

Cuvier married Mme. Davaucelle, a widow of a victim of the Revolution, in 1804. She already had four children from her previous

shape. In other instances, holes or cavities become filled with hardened mineral deposits. Another common type of fossil occurs when an organism is compressed within the Earth's crust. Over time the organism decomposes, and a thin layer of carbon is left behind. The last type of fossil results from an organism becoming trapped in a layer of sediment and the sediment hardening around it. If acidic liquid gains access to the organism, the organism can dissolve, leaving behind an imprint in the hardened sedimentary rock.

The scientific study of fossils is called *paleontology.* Paleontologists are interested in a variety of topics. For example, some paleontologists are interested in phylogenic relationships between all organisms, past and present. Others use fossil evidence to investigate geological time. The history of the Earth is divided into a set of geological time periods. Each division of time is characterized by a unique group of fossil remains, thus fossils can be used to determine when the rock layer in which they are embedded was formed. Paleontologists also use fossils to learn about tectonics, the movement of landmasses, throughout the history of the Earth.

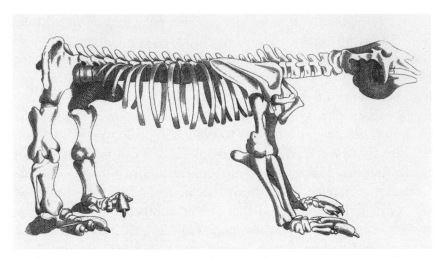

The discovery of a fossil skeleton of a large quadruped in Paraguay, South America, proved that species could become extinct. *(Library of Congress, Prints and Photographs Division [LC-USZ62-104286])*

marriage. Together they had four more children. Tragically, Cuvier was preceded in death by all of his children.

The nearby gypsum quarries of Montmartre and Mesnilmontant contained an abundance of well-preserved fossil remains. Cuvier appealed to a quarrier (someone who excavates stone from a quarry or pit) to bring him fossils uncovered during excavation. Cuvier had to draw on his expert skills to examine these fossils since they were embedded in hard plaster stone rather than loose sediment. Many of the fossils were from unknown species. He surmised that the Earth must have been previously crawling with *vertebrate* animals that no longer existed; in other words, animals became extinct.

Cuvier awed other scientists with his ability to identify organisms from only fragments of their skeletal remains. He claimed this was possible because organisms were well-integrated wholes. Their parts were not independent of one another. For example, if he found a tooth, he surmised the animal's diet from its construction. If it was a meat-eater, the animal's form would have a mobility that would permit it to capture its prey and strong jaws for crushing it. It would require a digestive system that could efficiently extract necessary nutrients from this type of food source. Each body part told enough of the full story that an anatomist familiar with the fundamental laws of comparative anatomy could reconstruct the entire organism with astounding accuracy. Cuvier went so far as to claim even the musculature could be reconstructed from imprints left on the bone. Since organisms are functionally integrated, Cuvier could use their structures to infer their habitat and even the physical history of the Earth at the time they roamed it.

Extinction and Catastrophism

Cuvier began to wonder why animals became extinct. By now he realized that the fossils of extinct organisms were not all the same age, which pointed to a series of revolutions. What happened in the geological past that interfered with these animals' survival? Why were their forms no longer sufficient for survival in the habitats that had previously supported their needs? Consequently, his interests shifted toward geology. He studied the material in which the fossils were found and tried to figure out what was happening at the time the strata were laid down. He was looking for keys to the geological history of Paris, clues to what might have happened that wiped out entire species. He appealed to other natural historians for collaboration. Meanwhile, he continued to publish prolifically on the bones of fossil animals. He identified several new but extinct species, including mammals similar to present-day otters, gazelles, hares, tapirs, opossums, and others.

Regarding Earth's history, Cuvier accepted the divisions of periods of time into epochs. He believed in a primary, universal, lifeless ocean prior to the formation of continents. Marine life appeared, then terrestrial life. The lack of human-type fossils and of intermediate fossils convinced him of the reality of extinction and creation of life in its original form. His lectures on geology contained few original ideas except when linked to fossil evidence. Even the idea of several cataclysmic revolutions of the Earth was not new.

Cuvier's training was in anatomy. A new interest in a field does not necessarily qualify one for productive study in that field. Cuvier was simply a biologist with an interest and natural talent in geology. In Alexandre Brongniart he found his complement, a geologist interested in biology. Brongniart had a background in mining engineering. Beginning in 1804, these two men undertook a study of the

Seine basin in northern France. They traveled around France examining the succession of strata, paying particular attention to the distinct groups of fossils embedded in each. Each fossil bed demonstrated that the surface of the Earth was not as it always had been.

In 1808, they presented a joint preliminary report to the Institute, *Mineral Geography of the Paris Region*. A fuller version was published in 1811, eventually leading to the most complete revision, *Geological Description of the Paris Region* (1822, 1835). Cuvier graciously gave the majority of credit to his associate for the efforts that resulted in this treatise. This work outlined the principles of paleontological *stratigraphy* and included a color-coded mineralogical map of the strata and detailed descriptions of nine different successive formations and embedded fossils. One goal was to give chronology to the Montmartre fossil beds. A significant finding was that there were major differences between the groups of fossils found in different beds. Each bed contained significantly different fossils than the beds above and below. Cuvier and Brongniart also reported finding both saltwater and freshwater organism remains in the same location. They suggested that fossils could be used to determine geological chronologies. For example, they could determine that a particular region was first submerged in salt water, then became dry land, then later was covered by freshwater. The strata may look similar, but if the fossils differed, the chronologies did as well. Cuvier also described some of the quadrupeds, or four-legged animals, that he found.

Sediments near the bottom of a stratigraphical column contained fossils from the oldest periods in geological time. Traveling upward toward more recently laid strata, Cuvier and Brongniart noticed that mammal remains suddenly appeared, though they were not remains of extant creatures, that is, creatures still in existence. As they continued ascending the column, they finally observed the remains of recognizable species. The succession was not gradual but erratic. Cuvier concluded that the breaks represented actual geological breaks and were indicative of major revolutions in Earth's history. These revolutions wiped out entire species, such that the species alive today do not represent the complete assortment of this

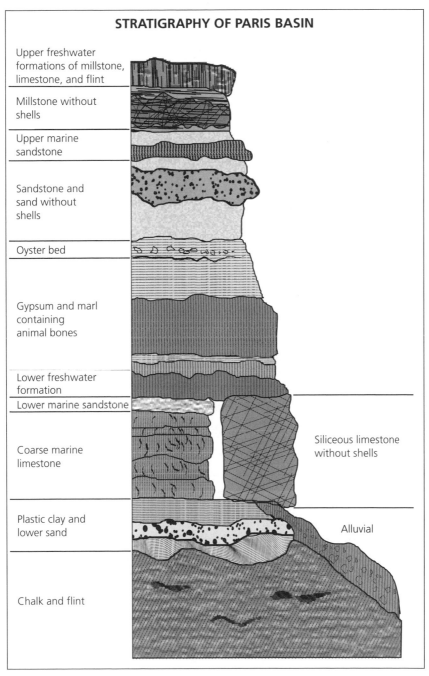

STRATIGRAPHY OF PARIS BASIN

Upper freshwater formations of millstone, limestone, and flint

Millstone without shells

Upper marine sandstone

Sandstone and sand without shells

Oyster bed

Gypsum and marl containing animal bones

Lower freshwater formation

Lower marine sandstone

Coarse marine limestone

Siliceous limestone without shells

Plastic clay and lower sand

Alluvial

Chalk and flint

Brongniart and Cuvier mapped the sequence of strata in the Paris basin.

planet's animals. Cuvier did not focus on whether new creations occurred after each catastrophe, though others thought this was a logical possibility. What is clear is that Cuvier did not believe gradual geological cycling was sufficient to explain the observations he made.

Cuvier was a catastrophist. Catastrophism suggests that certain geological features of the Earth's crust are the result of past cataclysmic events such as volcanic activity or a flood. Cuvier thought mass extinctions resulted from such geological catastrophes. The term *catastrophism* had not yet been used; instead, Cuvier referred to "global revolutions." He thought periodic revolutions reasonably explained why remains of saltwater and freshwater organisms were found at the same location and why there were apparent breaks in geological time according to rock strata. Though Cuvier did not specifically identify any revolutions with biblical events, catastrophism did not require that he abandon his Protestant upbringing. The biblical account of creation and the great flood was compatible with a catastrophic viewpoint—the great flood was simply the most recent great catastrophe. However, Cuvier's paleontological findings did convince him that creation must have occurred in many stages.

As far as extinction goes, how could anyone argue with Cuvier's claim that many former life-forms were no longer in existence? People did. They questioned why God would create something and then allow it to simply disappear. Some thought that the fossils were the remains of living organisms, just incorrectly identified. Others asserted that the species to which the fossil remains belonged had simply not yet been observed or identified by humans. Perhaps the species resided in an unexplored part of the world, they speculated.

By 1812, Cuvier's fossil research had almost ended. He collected, reordered, and reissued many of his previous related papers into the four-volume work, *Researches on Fossil Bones of Quadrupeds*. He added *Preliminary Discourse* to this work, which was accessible to the public. *Preliminary Discourse* summarized the evidence of global revolutions, geological structures and formations, research on fossil bones, their utility in uncovering Earth's history, and the extinction of life-forms. In 1826, this piece was published separately with a new title, *Discourse on the Revolution of the Surface of the Globe*.

Praised for its clarity, the booklet was ultimately reprinted many times in several languages. By the time Cuvier died it was in its sixth edition.

Still an Anatomist

Next Cuvier refocused on his original field of comparative anatomy. In 1817, he published a vast zoological composition, *The Animal Kingdom, Distributed According to Its Organization.* This work included descriptions of the entire animal kingdom. In it, he modified the classification system proposed by Swedish naturalist Carl Linnaeus. Cuvier recommended four major divisions of animal life: vertebrata, mollusca (including shellfish), articulata (including insects), and radiata (including echinoderms). This system may seem crude today, but at the time it emphasized the diversity of animal life, particularly the *invertebrates.*

In his 1809 *Zoological Philosophy*, French naturalist Jean-Baptiste de Monet de Lamarck suggested that living things transmutated. Their forms gradually changed to become better adapted to their environment and these changes were passed on to the next generation. According to Lamarck, animals were becoming more and more complex. At the time it was popular to believe in the stability of life-forms—each creature existed as God originally had created it. The form of each creature was not subject to mutation. Change would not only violate moral law, but also decrease the ability of an animal to survive in the particular environment for which it was divinely suited. Besides, if animals were mutable, then the entire science of taxonomy would have no basis. Étienne Geoffroy Saint-Hiliare, who had initially written Cuvier inducing him to move to Paris, and who himself believed that animals were subject to change, brought Cuvier some mummified ibises (a type of bird) from Egypt in 1802. After studying them, Cuvier found that though the mummified birds were more than 3,000 years old, their morphology was identical to current ibises. At the time, 3,000 years was considered a very long time. Most people believed the Earth itself was only about 6,000 years old. Cuvier thought that if they had not changed in 3,000 years, they were never going to change.

When two of Geoffroy's associates tried to demonstrate that a link existed between cephalopods (invertebrates) and fish (vertebrates), Cuvier interfered. This eventually led to a huge public debate between the former collaborators and friends, Geoffroy and Cuvier, at the Royal Academy of Sciences in Paris in 1830. The issue was whether form determined mechanical function or the converse, function dictated form. Geoffroy believed that all vertebrates had a common form of basic organization, with only slight modifications. He claimed that vestigial organs such as the appendix demonstrated that all vertebrates originally shared a common ancestral form. He thought that if structures were connected in the same manner, then differences in size or shape were not so important. Cuvier responded that similarities in form were simply the result of similar functions and believed in the integration of parts into functional wholes. Today anatomists accept both concepts depending on the structures and species that are being compared. For example, the wings of a bird and the wings of an insect both allow the organisms function of flight, but these two types of animals do not share a common structural archetypical ancestor. These structures are considered analogous. On the other hand, the wings of birds and the wings of a bat do share a common vertebrate structural ancestor; they are more closely linked evolutionarily. Being derived from a common ancestral structure, the structures are referred to as homologous.

The Natural History of Fish was another enormous zoological work by Cuvier. Written in collaboration with Achille Valenciennes, it summarized all of the content knowledge of the field of *ichthyology*, the study of fish. The first volume was published in 1828, with eight more being completed prior to Cuvier's death. The 22nd and final volume was published in 1849. The classification system contained in this work remains the basis of modern ichthyologic classification.

Cuvier's Legacy

In May 1832, Cuvier suffered an attack of paralysis and died within a few days. His legacies include his library, which boasted more than 19,000 volumes and thousands of pamphlets. In addition, he had increased the collections at the Musée from a few hundred to more than 13,000 specimens, all arranged according to his own classification system. Cuvier is most remembered for catastrophism and for establishing the reality of extinction of past life-forms. However, his contributions in the form of progress reports on science and scientific biographies submitted in the capacity of permanent secretary to the Institute are also noteworthy.

Constantly striving to overcome his humble beginnings, Cuvier was reported to be somewhat arrogant, hurried, and anxious to receive flattery. He did achieve prominence during his lifetime and was honored appropriately with many appointments and titles. He was not handsome but was admired for his intelligence, though he was too stubborn to open his mind concerning the variability of species. Because of this, once the theory of evolution by means of *natural selection* became widely accepted, Cuvier's reputation diminished. However, he will always hold a place in scientific history for bridging the gap between the Earth sciences and the life sciences by founding the science of vertebrate paleontology.

CHRONOLOGY

1769	Georges Cuvier is born on August 23 in Montbéliard
1784–88	Studies at Caroline University in Stuttgart
1788	Begins private tutoring in Normandy
1795	Starts teaching animal anatomy at the Musée National d'Histoire Naturelle in Paris and is appointed professor of zoology at the Écoles Centrales
1796	Becomes member of the Class of Physical Sciences of the Institut de France and presents research identifying an extinct animal, *Elephas primigenius*
1800	Becomes professor of natural history at the Collège de France
1800–05	Publishes five volumes of *Lessons in Comparative Anatomy*
1802	Is appointed professor of comparative anatomy at the Musée National d'Histoire Naturelle

1803	Becomes permanent secretary of physical sciences of the Institut de France
1804	Begins geological research on the succession of strata with Alexandre Brongniart
1808	Is appointed university counselor by Napoleon
1808–11	Publishes *Mineral Geography of the Paris Region,* which was rewritten and expanded into *Geological Description of the Paris Region* (1822, 1835)
1809–13	Travels to Italy, the Netherlands, and Germany to reorganize the higher education systems
1812	Publishes *Researches on Fossil Bones of Quadrupeds*
1814	Becomes councillor of state
1817	Publishes *The Animal Kingdom, Distributed According to Its Organization*
1819–32	Presides over the Interior Department of the Council of State
1826	Publishes *Discourse on the Revolution of the Surface of the Globe,* a separate printing of the *Preliminary Discourse* from *Researches on Fossil Bones of Quadrupeds*
1828	Publishes first of 22 volumes of *The Natural History of Fish*
1830	Debates publicly with Étienne Geoffroy Saint-Hiliare
1832	Dies on May 13 in Paris, France

FURTHER READING

Cuvier, M. le Baron. *Discourse on the Revolutionary Upheavals on the Surface of the Globe and on the Changes Which They Have Produced in the Animal Kingdom.* Available online. URL: http://www.mala.bc.ca/~johnstoi/cuvier-e.htm. Accessed January 15, 2005. English translation of Cuvier's most famous work, with extensive notes and references.

Gillispie, Charles C., ed. *Dictionary of Scientific Biography.* Vol. 3. New York: Scribner, 1970–76. Good source for facts concerning personal backgrounds and scientific accomplishments but assumes reader has basic knowledge of science.

Rudwick, Martin J. S. *Georges Cuvier, Fossil Bones, and Geological Catastrophes: New Translations and Interpretations of the Primary Texts.* Chicago: University of Chicago Press, 1997. Includes modern translations of geological works, with introductory comments and background information for each entry.

University of California–Berkeley Museum of Paleontology. "Georges Cuvier (1769–1832)." Available online. URL: http://www.ucmp.berkeley.edu/history/cuvier.html. Accessed January 15, 2005. Standard biography.

William Smith

(1769–1839)

William Smith formulated the principle of fossil succession and created the first large-scale geological map. *(Science Photo Library/Photo Researchers, Inc.)*

Creation of the World's First Geological Map

The anticipation that accompanies the arrival of a wrapped present compels some people to try to figure out what is inside. Taking note of the size and structure of the container helps to pare down the possible contents. The next step often involves tapping the box or probing it for a more precise shape than the package obviously reveals. At the turn of the 19th century, one man was able to see through Earth's wrappings of soil and vegetation to predict what was underneath. William Smith was a self-taught surveyor who recognized the regular succession of strata across England and proposed that lithologically similar rock beds could be distinguished by the groups of characteristic fossils embedded within. Using this information, he created the world's first large-scale *geological map* of an entire country.

Pound Stones

William Smith was born on March 23, 1769, to John and Ann Smith of Churchill, Oxfordshire, England. He was the eldest of four children. John was a blacksmith and a mechanic, but he died when William was only eight years old. Ann remarried a few years later. William learned writing and arithmetic at the village school, which he attended until he was 11 years old. As a child he was attracted to the pound stones that he found on Oxfordshire fields. These were round, dome-shaped stones that weighed approximately one pound and were used as a standard weight measure by dairymaids. Sometimes they had an interesting pattern shaped like a five-point star. It turns out that these were fossilized remains of sea urchins. William also collected pundibs, spherical-shaped rocks the size of acorns that actually were the remains of *terebratulids*, a type of *brachiopod*. A suitable substitute for marbles, they were merely play toys to young William, though hindsight shows they were an unrecognized symbol of his future achievements.

Career as Surveyor

William lived with an uncle who treated him decently. Yet William, who continued studying on his own after leaving the village school, had to ask to borrow from his inheritance to purchase books. One such book was *The Art of Measuring* by Daniel Fenning. One day when he was 18, he happened to be walking around town carrying this book. A man named Edward Webb was visiting Oxfordshire. He was a professional surveyor, someone who determined boundaries of areas and measured land elevations using geometry and trigonometry. Webb needed an apprentice to help him divide some farming fields and hired William as an assistant.

Smith learned about the soil and rocks of Oxfordshire and the methods of surveying quickly. Within a few months he could skillfully use a *pantograph*, a *theodolite*, dividers, and a great steel chain, all tools for geographical surveying. By summer 1788, Smith was doing his own work. He traveled with Webb and eventually moved in with Webb's family, who lived 10 miles away at Stow-on-the-Wold. As he traveled, he kept diaries of his observations, especially geological findings.

In 1791, Smith traveled to Somerset to do a valuation survey in the village of Stowey, near Bath. He ended up staying there and working for Webb for a few years, getting to know the terrain and making contacts with the residents. One influential woman he met was Lady Elizabeth Jones, whose land he originally visited to survey. He rented a farmhouse from her called Rugborne, on the eastern side of High Littleton. This estate later became known as the birthplace of geology.

Somerset was a coal mining community, and Lady Jones was the director of the High Littleton Coal Company. Under her employment, Smith surveyed, planned, and drained land. In 1792, his main work site was the Mearns Pit. The first time Smith went into that mine, he was puzzled by what he observed. As he descended into the mine, he passed grass, gravel, and topsoil, and then a more solid rock layer consisting of limestone, *marlstone*, and *shales*. Below this rocky layer was an abrupt transition. The color suddenly changed from reddish green to grayish brown, and there was a surprising, deep, downward slope. This layer was warped and all broken-up, in sharp contrast to the nicely laid out horizontal sheets of varying thicknesses in the upper layers.

Approximately 300 million years ago, the European and African tectonic plates collided with each other, forming *Pangaea*, an enormous former supercontinent composed of all the existing continents. The resulting compression and folding persisted for millions of years, forming many unique geological structures throughout Britain. This process was termed the *Variscan Orogeny*, and it left an unordered mess of pre-Permian rocks. It also made coal mining difficult in north Somerset since rocks containing useful coal were deposited during the Upper Carboniferous period, 290–310 million years ago.

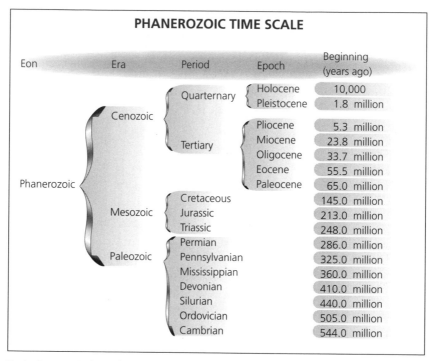

PHANEROZOIC TIME SCALE

Eon	Era	Period	Epoch	Beginning (years ago)
Phanerozoic	Cenozoic	Quarternary	Holocene	10,000
			Pleistocene	1.8 million
		Tertiary	Pliocene	5.3 million
			Miocene	23.8 million
			Oligocene	33.7 million
			Eocene	55.5 million
			Paleocene	65.0 million
	Mesozoic	Cretaceous		145.0 million
		Jurassic		213.0 million
		Triassic		248.0 million
	Paleozoic	Permian		286.0 million
		Pennsylvanian		325.0 million
		Mississippian		360.0 million
		Devonian		410.0 million
		Silurian		440.0 million
		Ordovician		505.0 million
		Cambrian		544.0 million

Each time period on the geological timescale is represented by a unique system of rock types.

During his time in the mines, Smith made other astute observations. For example, he found the same pattern in mine after mine. From top to bottom, this pattern was sandstone, *siltstone*, mudstone, nonmarine band, marine band, coal, seat Earth, and then back to sandstone, in a cyclical pattern. Particular seams of coal were always located in the same relative position. He also noticed that all sedimentary rocks laid down at the same time were similar and that the same fossil types appeared in the same stratigraphical order. Smith began to view geology as more of a science, and his interest grew.

Smith wondered if this predictability would be true elsewhere. Could these patterns be applied to other rocks that lay below the ground but miles away? What about to rocks above the ground, such as in mountains? Could one use this sort of information to predict where certain rock types lay? He wanted to gather more data so he could begin answering these questions.

Meanwhile, the miners were fretful. Across the Avon River, the Welsh were building a canal to help transport their coal. Somerset

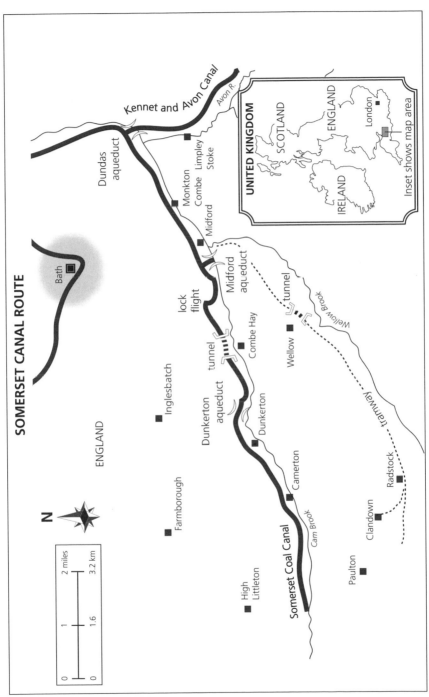

As an engineer for the Somerset Coal Canal, Smith was responsible for selecting the route for the canal to carry coal from the mines to the market.

could not compete for coal sales if they could not move their coal efficiently, so they decided to build a canal as well. A surveyor was needed to determine the best route for what was to be called the Somerset Coal Canal. The canal eventually connected Limpley Stoke, at a junction with a larger canal, to Camerton, where the coal was.

A Scotsman named John Rennie initially signed on to make the survey, but he was too busy. Lady Jones suggested Smith as an apprentice. In 1793, Smith started inspecting the structure of the land to choose a route for the canal that would be easy to dig and retain water. This was a wonderful opportunity for him to collect geological information from the rock exposed by the digging. He eventually recommended that two parallel canals be built, a northerly Dunkerton Line and a southerly Radstock Line. This allowed him to examine the geology of even more land areas. He noticed a uniform dip to the rocks between Dunkerton and Midford. This taught him that strata did not always exist as horizontal lines. He also observed that there was a distinctive sequence to the rock layers and was anxious to learn if his ideas and observations applied to the entire nation.

In early 1794, Smith traveled to London to witness before Parliament in order to obtain authorization to build the canal. This was simply a bureaucratic process necessary before commencing with the project. He had a lot of spare time while in London, and he spent it at libraries and bookstores trying to learn if anyone else had published anything similar to the ideas that were forming in his mind. He was unsuccessful but still worried that someone else might be developing his same ideas.

The Birth of Stratigraphy

Smith took a carriage trip with two other members of the canal committee later that year. The purpose of the 900-mile (1,448-km) trip over England and Wales was to see how others were building canals. While on this excursion, he continually jumped off the stagecoach to take samples of rock and fossils and took frequent notes of geological observations. He commented to his companions that he could tell from the landscaping just what type of rock lay underneath. He demonstrated this skill to the older men, who were no doubt amused by his enthusiasm.

Smith was becoming quite skilled at identifying different strata, but some strata looked very similar. If rock layers were deposited under the same conditions, even if during different time periods, they can look alike. Likewise, rock layers that were deposited at the same time and were of similar composition can look different due to physical disturbances such as volcanic activity or sweeping currents. In one instance, Smith had observed separate outcrops of limestone that looked very similar but were separated by great distances, representing long periods of time. In addition, his knowledge of *dip* and *strike* had convinced him they were in fact different strata from different time periods. Dip is the angle by which a rock layer deviates from the horizontal plane, and strike is the direction 90 degrees to the dip. So, how could one distinguish these rock layers? After years of careful examination of the terrain across England, Smith formulated his principle of *fossil succession*, which he memorialized by writing in his journal of 1796.

The principle of fossil succession states that the sequence of fossils in rock strata is so regular that fossils can be used to identify the rocks in which they are embedded. Fossils can be used to establish the time sequence by which the rocks were laid. This was a new concept for geologists in the early 1800s, but today it is a basic principle of stratigraphy. Around the same time, Georges Cuvier and Alexandre Brongniart were also recognizing the utility of fossils in geological chronologies.

In 1798, Smith purchased a home near Bath called the Tucking Mill. Bath was uniquely suited for geological study since the Middle Jurassic rock outcrop was blatantly exposed. Many strata were apparent, including outcrops of rocks spanning several time periods. While living there, he created what is technically considered the first true geological map, a circular map with a five-mile (8-km) radius and Bath at its center. Smith noted the locations of different fossil types and used dip and strike information to estimate locations of various strata. Significantly, he used color to specifically depict the locations of *oolite* (yellow), Lias (dirty blue), and red marls (brick red).

Mary Anning

During the two-month excursion across England in 1794, Smith sketched a rough map of the Lower Jurassic sea cliffs of Lyme Regis. This small, seaside town on the Dorset coast was especially suited for fossil hunting. Due to the angle, the Triassic rocks are buried under the sea, but the older Jurassic rocks made of thick clays and thin limestone are exposed. These rocks were deposited in a sea that was packed with marine life. Lyme Regis also happened to be the future home of Mary Anning (1799–1847), a famous fossil collector. Though it is unlikely that Anning and Smith ever met, they shared an interest in these cliffs that were particularly rich in fossils. Fossils were to become Smith's key to predicting the *stratification* of England's underground.

Mary's life was destined to be unusual when at age 15 months she survived a lightning strike. Her family suffered many other tragedies, including the deaths of her father and eight of her brothers and sisters. As a girl, she spent a lot of time searching for fossils on the shores underneath the cliffs near her home. After her father's death, Mary's family was poor. They sold fossils and other curiosities to supplement their meager welfare assistance. When she was only 12, she found the fossil remains of a 17-foot-long ichthyosaur embedded in a rock that had fallen from the cliffs onto the shore. It took her almost one year to dig the specimen out, and no one knew what it was. Some called it a crocodile, others a fish. Scientists later

Smith was suddenly fired from the Somerset Canal Company in 1799 for an unknown reason. He worked as an independent mineral surveyor and drainage engineer for the next two decades. His expertise was in constant demand, and he made decent money, but unfortunately, most of his earnings were spent on a project that occupied him until 1815, the construction of a large-scale geological map.

determined it was from the Mesozoic era, which occurred between 65 and 48 million years ago. The Annings sold the fossil skeleton for a sum that fed the family for six months. Anning later unearthed several more ichthyosaurs, suggesting that there were several different species. Most of the recognition for the discovery of ichthyosaurs went to the people who purchased the fossils Anning found.

In 1823, she came across another amazing discovery, a skeleton about nine feet (2.7 m) long and six feet (1.8 m) wide, with a small head, long neck, and the body of a turtle, but no shell. This creature was named a plesiosaur. Later it was determined to have lived during the middle of the Mesozoic era. The discovery earned Anning a reputation of being a superior fossil hunter. She continued to collect specimens and sold them to famous noblemen and scientists, allowing her to purchase a new home for her family in 1826.

Anning was the first to recognize that coprolites were fossilized dung. In 1828, she found the near perfect remains of a flying reptile. This was the first pterosaur, or "winged lizard," also from the Mesozoic era. The next year, she found an unknown fish species, *Squaloraja*, that resembles an intermediate between sharks and rays. In late 1830, she discovered the *Plesiosaurus macrocephalus*, or plesiosaur with a bigger head.

Mary Anning died in 1847 of breast cancer. A few months before she died, she was made an honorary member of the Geological Society of London. Many of her fossil finds are displayed in museums across Europe. Though some claim she earned her fame by luck, her persistence, skill, and recognition of unusual and important finds led Anning to become one of the greatest fossilists ever known.

Smith was elected to the Bath Agricultural Society in 1796. This association led to many connections that had later influences on Smith's life and accomplishments. Two encouraging members, Reverend Benjamin Richardson of Farleigh and Reverend Joseph Townsend of Pewsey, were also fossil collectors. One night in 1799, after dining together at the home of Townsend, the clerics pulled out some paper and wrote, as Smith dictated, a list of strata. This was in the form of a table that included information not only on the succession of 23 strata from chalk to coal, but also on their thicknesses, lithological characteristics, and distinguishing types of embedded fossils. They made three copies of the table that night, one for each of them, with the understanding that the men would recopy and disseminate this information to whomever was interested. Years later, Smith heard that copies of this table were being distributed on different continents.

In 1801, Richardson suggested that Smith write a prospectus, outlining his intent to publish a work on the natural order of strata in England and Wales. He obtained the sponsorship of Sir Joseph Banks, the president of the Royal Society of London for this project. Years passed, however, and no progress was made. Smith was too busy working, trying to make enough money to pay his mortgages.

In 1805, Smith had leased a large house in London. Being of common birth and never formally educated, he felt it was important to keep up appearances of success in order to obtain respectable employment and sponsorship; however, he still owned his Tucking Mill estate. In addition, he had made a bad investment a few years earlier. He took out a second mortgage on Tucking Mill to invest in a quarry for the excavation of oolitic limestone, a popular building material. Unfortunately, times were bad, and in the early 1800s people stopped building altogether. Furthermore, the quality of the stone was inferior. Smith also rented an office in Bath, serving as his base for a brief partnership he had in a firm, Smith and Cruse, Land Surveyors. At the expense of his long-awaited mapping project, he furiously toiled away just trying to make ends meet.

In the midst of this, Smith got married. His 17-year-old bride, Mary Ann, was uneducated, often physically ill, and eventually became mentally deranged, adding to Smith's troubles. In 1807, he became the guardian of his orphaned nephew, John Phillips. John later became Smith's assistant and then a notable geologist, but at the time he was another financial burden.

One notorious achievement by Smith in 1810 was repairing the famous Bath hot springs that had failed mysteriously and were drying out. Smith's expertise was called upon, and he soon found that a bone from a ruminant was clogging the passage of water to the springs. The bone had become lodged and then covered in crystals. Smith removed it, and the springs flowed even better than originally.

The World's First Geological Map

John Cary, a highly regarded English cartographer, agreed to publish Smith's map in 1812. A topographical map was engraved, on top of which Smith added his geological information. The actual construction of the map was quite a task itself, involving 16 engraved plates and three years to accomplish. The data collection and assimilation of the information took Smith 14 years to complete. The completed map, *A Delineation of the Strata of England and Wales, with Part of Scotland*, was published in 1815 with a 50-page textual explanation.

The map was slightly larger than eight by six feet (2.4 by 1.8 m) with the scale being five miles (8 km) to one inch (2.54 cm). One striking feature was the color. Smith used a variety of shades to depict certain types of rock: gray for *Tertiary* outcrops, blue-green for chalk, brown for Coral Rag and Carstone, yellow for oolites, blue for Lias, and red for Red Ground. Not only was the use of color original, but he also colored the base of each rock formation darker than its top. Thus, if one stood back, an immediate pattern was apparent. This piece of work became a classic in cartography. Modern geological maps use the same principles and even the same color scheme that Smith used almost two hundred years ago.

Four hundred copies were made, but they sold poorly, partly due to George Bellas Greenough, one of the original founders of the Geological Society of London, a small, elite club of rich intellectuals. Though Smith was hurt by the lack of inclusion in their society, in 1808, he had invited them to view his impressive fossil collection, which was carefully organized by chronological succession and beautifully displayed on a series of sloping shelves meant to represent the sequence of strata. The visit of the Geological Society was a disappointing one. Smith neither received the praise he deserved nor the invitation to join the Geological Society that he so desperately craved. Little did he know that the president of the Geological Society was not only impressed but also jealous.

A Delineation of the Strata of England and Wales, with Part of Scotland
was hand-colored, with different colors representing different rock types.
*(Reproduced by permission of the British Geological Survey. © NERC. All
rights reserved. IPR/53-42C)*

Greenough was about to embark on a mission of scientific pilfering that would be personally and professionally catastrophic to Smith.

Greenough announced the intention of the Geological Society to publish a geological map of England, similar to Smith's. Potential buyers of Smith's map decided to wait until Greenough's map was published rather than buy Smith's map. After all, Smith's did not have the backing of the Geological Society, and Greenough's promised to be cheaper. When the map did come out in 1819, it did not fare much better than Smith's map, nor did it contain any new information. Later Greenough was forced to admit that he stole much of Smith's work in constructing his map. In a ridiculous effort to make amends, Greenough apologized and presented a copy of his map to Smith.

Financial troubles intensified, and Smith was forced to sell his extensive fossil collection to the British Museum (the present-day Natural History Museum of London). In hopes of earning a little money, Smith published *Strata Identified by Organized Fossils* (1816) and *Stratigraphical System of Organized Fossils Part I* (1817). The latter was a catalogue of the collection now owned by the museum. Neither sold well, and he continued creating and publishing geological maps of several counties in England (1819–24). He also released *A Geological Section from London to Snowdon* (1817), showing the relative thicknesses and arrangements of rocks. In 1819, unfortunately, his financial difficulties became too great. He was sent to debtor's prison for 11 weeks, during which time he lost his home and his few remaining personal belongings. He would have lost his papers and maps too, but an anonymous friend purchased and returned them to Smith. After his release, he gathered his sickly wife and his nephew and moved away from London, where he had been so horribly treated, into obscurity, where he remained for the next 12 years.

The family traveled to Yorkshire, where Smith enjoyed lecturing on geology, but he had to give this up due to poor health. He settled in Scarborough from 1824 to 1828 and continued to study geology. He also designed a museum and helped with the town water supply.

Respected at Last

Sir John Vanden Bempde Johnstone hired Smith as his land steward in Hackness in 1828. Johnstone was a member of the Geological Society and a fossil collector himself. He was aware of Smith's accomplishments, and with the assistance of a friend, he championed for an annuity to be purchased for the aging geologist.

In 1831, Smith was awarded the first Wollaston Medal by the Geological Society of London in recognition of his research into the mineral structure of the Earth. In return, Smith presented the Geological Society with his original table of 23 strata (1799), his colored geological map of Bath and the surrounding area (1799), and an original rough sketch of his geological masterpiece (1801). He received his gold medal the next year followed by a government pension. Trinity College in Dublin awarded him an honorary doctorate degree in 1835.

Smith's last job was serving as part of a committee selected by the government to choose the new building material for the British House of Parliament, as the old building had burned down in 1834. The committee selected a magnesium limestone from a quarry in Derbyshire. The supply ran short, and a quick substitution had to be found. The substitute stone turned out to be unsuitable. One wonders if Smith might have recognized this and corrected the error before it was too late if he had lived longer. Within 10 years, the exterior of the buildings deteriorated.

On the way to a British Association meeting in Birmingham, Smith stopped to visit a friend in Northampton. He caught a cold that turned fatal. The father of English geology died on August 28, 1839. He was buried nearby in Saint Peter's Church.

Smith freely shared his knowledge of England's geology. His geological maps were practically applied to the fields of mining, agriculture, road building, water draining, and canal building. His 1815 map of England and Wales is considered a milestone in geological cartography. Though Smith's major accomplishments went unnoticed by the scientific community initially, Smith's contributions to geography and biostratigraphy were just beginning to be recognized at the time of his death. In 1865, the Geological Society added Smith's name to Greenough's map, rightfully acknowledging his intellectual contribution. The Geological Society and the Oxford Museum display busts of Smith, and signposts and plaques adorn his former residences. Since 1977, the Geological Society has awarded the William Smith Medal for contributions to applied and economic aspects of geology. The man who revealed his vision of the underworld has finally received the recognition he deserves.

CHRONOLOGY

1769	William Smith is born on March 23 in Churchill, Oxfordshire, England
1787	Becomes assistant surveyor to Edward Webb
1791	Travels to north Somerset to survey and value an estate
1793–99	Plans route and supervises digging of the Somerset Coal Canal in southeastern England
1796	Discovers that rock beds with similar compositions can be distinguished by their fossil assemblages
1799	Dictates list of strata and characteristic fossils of Bath to two clergymen and begins a series of engineering jobs all over Britain
1806	Publishes book on irrigation and water meadows, *Observations on the Utility, Form, and Management of Water Meadows*. Shows fossil collection to members of the new Geological Society of London
1812	Completes geological map, which is accepted by publisher John Cary
1815	Publishes geological map, *A Delineation of the Strata of England and Wales, with Part of Scotland*. Begins selling fossil collection to the British Museum due to money troubles
1816–19	Publishes *Strata Identified by Organized Fossils*
1817	Publishes *Stratigraphical System of Organized Fossils Part I*

1819–24	Publishes geological maps of 21 English counties
1831	Receives the first Wollaston Medal of the Geological Society of London for outstanding achievement in geology
1839	Dies on August 28 in Northampton, England

FURTHER READING

Gillispie, Charles C., ed. *Dictionary of Scientific Biography*. Vol. 12. New York: Scribner, 1970–76. Good source for facts concerning personal backgrounds and scientific accomplishments but assumes reader has basic knowledge of science.

Olson, Richard, ed. *Biographical Encyclopedia of Scientists*. Vol. 5. New York: Marshall Cavendish, 1998. Clear, concise summary of major events in the scientists' lives.

William "Strata" Smith on the Web. Department of Earth Sciences, University of New Hampshire (UNH). Available online. URL: http://www.unh.edu/esci/wmsmith.html. Revised March 20, 2004. Includes three of Smith's original publications, with explanatory notes written by UNH professor emeritus Dr. Cecil Schneer.

Winchester, Simon. *The Map That Changed the World*. Rockland, Mass.: Wheeler, 2001. Recounts Smith's entire life story, including personal information and scientific visions.

7

Sir Charles Lyell

(1797–1875)

Sir Charles Lyell's pioneering work, *Principles of Geology*, thrust uniformitarianism into the geological mainstream. *(Library of Congress, Prints and Photographs Division [LC-USZ62-123180])*

The Gradual Nature of Earth's Processes

In the early 1830s, Sir Charles Lyell authored the pioneering work, *Principles of Geology*, a textbook that propelled uniformitarianism into the geological mainstream and is now considered a classic in the field. With this single influential work, he firmly established geology as a science by convincing geologists to study the present to learn about the past. Since people cannot directly observe past processes, they must compare the results of those processes (for example, fossils, mountains, and lavas) with modern geological phenomena currently forming by processes that are observable. Trained as a lawyer, Lyell's verbal skills were impressive, and he was a persuasive writer. Though the theme of *Principles* was not novel, Lyell reintroduced Scottish geologist James Hutton's ideas with a preponderance of supporting evidence that he gathered during numerous geological excursions across Europe and North America. He also dared to profess that humans were much older than creationists believed and named several geological eras: Eocene, Miocene, and older and newer Pliocene.

Preference of Geology over Law

Charles Lyell was the oldest of 10 siblings, born to the former Frances Smith on November 14, 1797, at the family estate, Kinnordy, at Kirriemuir, in the county of Angus, Scotland. His father, Charles senior, was a wealthy lawyer who enjoyed collecting rare plants. His family moved to Hampshire, England, when Charles was an infant. At the age of seven, he was sent to the first of several English schools and graduated at the top of his class in June 1815. When he was 11 years old, he suffered a bout of pleurisy and while recovering he took up the hobby of insect collecting, using his father's library books to identify them. *Entomology* (the study of insects) spawned a more general interest in the natural sciences that persisted throughout his life.

Lyell entered Exeter College at Oxford University in January 1816 to study Greek, Latin, and the writings of Aristotle. Having already read *Introduction to Geology* (1813) by Robert Bakewell, he was anxious to attend the mineralogy and geology lectures given by William Buckland. The English geology professor was a neptunist, meaning he supported the theories of German geologist Abraham Gottlob Werner, who proposed the then commonly accepted idea that all rocks on the Earth were formed from a vast, ancient ocean that completely covered the planet and shaped the structure of its surface with swirling, turbulent waters. While at Oxford, Lyell began making geological excursions, a practice that would continue throughout his lifetime. In 1817, Lyell studied the column-shaped formations of basalt on the island of Staffa, Scotland. German geologist Leopold von Buch had proposed that Fingal's Cave on Staffa was formed by erosion of a dike of soft lava, but Lyell observed that the basalt columns of the cave's roof had broken ends, demonstrating Buch's theory to be false. While traveling to France, Switzerland, and Italy with his family in 1818, Lyell witnessed the effect of glaciers in the Alps and recognized an age sequence in the succession of rock exposures he observed.

In 1819, Lyell became a fellow of both the Geological Society and the Linnean Society of London. In December of that year, he received a bachelor of arts in the classics from Oxford University. At his father's request, Lyell entered Lincoln's Inn to study law, but he also continued to study geology. He was admitted to the bar in 1822, but poor eyesight caused his eyes to swell and hurt frequently, making legal reading difficult. The Geological Society elected him joint secretary in 1823, demonstrating that he was accepted as a geologist by his peers.

Uniformity Revealed

He visited Paris that year and met several famous scientists including Georges Cuvier, Alexander von Humboldt, and Constant Prévost. The alternating layers of marine and freshwater formations in the Paris basin intrigued Lyell, and he realized that minor changes to a geological barrier could explain the pattern. In 1824, Lyell accompanied Buckland on a trip through Scotland during which he pondered the Parallel Roads of Glen Roy, admired the granite veins of Glen Tilt, and studied limestone and marl deposits in small freshwater lakes in Bailie. He read his first paper, "On a Recent Formation of Freshwater Limestone in Forfarshire," to the Geological Society in December of that year, followed by more on Tertiary exposures of the Hampshire coast of England. In 1826, an article he published in the *Quarterly Review*, titled "Transactions of the Geological Society of London," summarized the current knowledge and major areas of investigation in geology. While composing this review, he began to believe that ordinary geological forces such as earthquakes and volcanoes could explain unusual phenomena such as the presence of sedimentary strata formed on

William Buckland

William Buckland was born at Axminster, Devonshire, England, on March 12, 1784. In 1798, he enrolled at St. Mary's College in Winchester, and then he won a scholarship to study geology at Corpus Christi College at Oxford. He earned a bachelor of arts degree in 1804. After becoming a fellow in 1808, he traveled across England to survey geological sites and collect samples. He became a professor of mineralogy at Oxford in 1813, and the first professor of geology in 1819. The Royal Society of London elected him to membership in 1818.

Having identified and named the first species of dinosaur, Buckland initiated a new line of paleontological research. In Stonesfield, he found teeth, jaws, and limb bones that he concluded were from a large, carnivorous, extinct reptile that he named *Megalosaurus*. At the time in 1824, dinosaurs were not yet recognized as a distinct group of reptiles, and the term *dinosaur* had not yet been coined.

the ocean floor but found on mountain summits. The Royal Society of London elected Lyell a fellow in 1826. He practiced law until 1827, but then gave it up to devote his career to geology.

He continued making geological excursions, including trips to France, Italy, and Scotland, collecting data wherever he visited. One journey in 1828 that affected his views about geological processes brought him to France, Germany, and Italy with Roderick Murchison, a Scottish geologist. In central France, Lyell found analogies between the geological past and formations currently developing. Again, he thought modern processes must resemble those that shaped ancient formations. The revelation struck him that the appearance of strata was determined by the conditions when it was laid, not just by age. Similar conditions in the present day could replicate a layer with characteristics in common with an

Another well-known investigation of Buckland's concerned his finding of fossil remains of extinct animals in a cavern of Kirkdale, in Yorkshire. Many scientists believed that rolling flood waters carried the remains of perished animals from their tropical habitats to the cavern, but Buckland observed gnawed and splintered bones, some with flesh still attached, alongside a great number of hyena remains, suggesting that hyenas inhabited the cave before the flood and killed their prey in that location. He thought mud covered and protected the remains before the flood waters came.

Buckland's most famous work, *Relics of the Deluge,* published in 1823, established his reputation as a respected geologist. The book presented geological evidence supporting the biblical account of a great flood, or deluge. He claimed that *siliceous* (containing silica) pebbles scattered across the countryside were deposited there by running waters. After observing smooth gouges in rock across Great Britain, he later claimed that Scotland and England were once covered in colossal sheets of glacial ice.

Buckland became dean of Westminster in 1845 and did not have much time for geological research afterward. He had served as president of the Geological Society of London in 1824 and in 1840, and the society awarded him their Wollaston Medal in 1848. Buckland died on August 24, 1856.

ancient stratum; thus, modern conditions and geological processes must resemble those of the past.

In Italy, he saw layers of lava exposed in the mountain walls of Etna, fossils of living species buried at its base, and younger uplifted strata with large percentages of extant (currently existing) species. These observations led to his conclusion that the volcanic mountain had been formed relatively recently, layer by layer. Accruing evidence caused him to doubt the neptunist doctrine, and he observed more physical support for the vulcanists, who believed that volcanic activity was responsible for the major changes in the construction of the Earth's surface. Cuvier believed that life on Earth was periodically destroyed through the violent actions of catastrophic events such as floods. Lyell rejected this idea of catastrophism. Instead, he believed that geological changes were caused gradually by ordinary geological

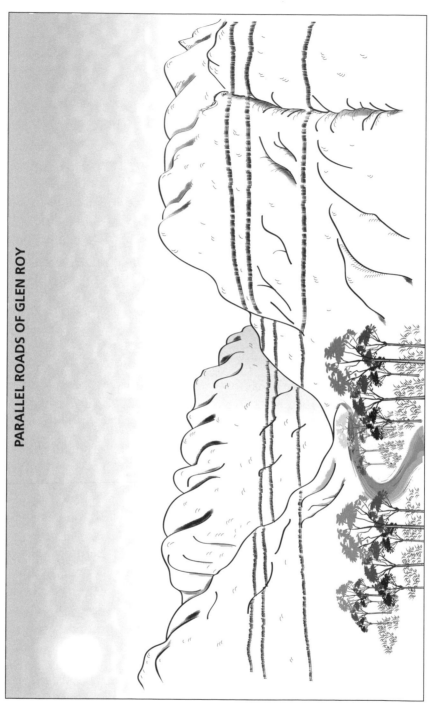

PARALLEL ROADS OF GLEN ROY

In the West Highlands of Scotland, the Parallel Roads of Glen Roy and the adjacent valleys are remnant shorelines of a huge glacial lake that filled the Glen as the last ice age drew to an end more than 10,000 years ago.

processes, a theory called uniformitarianism, proposed by Scottish geologist James Hutton in 1785. Lyell believed that the steady accumulation of changes from earthquakes and volcanic activity caused the elevation and disturbances found in the sedimentary rocks. He imagined that geological processes he directly observed also occurred in the past, forming analogous structures.

Principles and Elements

Geologists of the time were prepared to reject Werner's ideas for Hutton's, but they needed a push. They were ready to accept that basalt was of igneous origin but more hesitant to accept uniformity of geological processes of the past and the present and of uniform gradual rates of change. Lyell published *Principles of Geology: An Attempt to Explain the Former Changes in the Earth's Surface by Reference to Causes Now in Operation*, which appeared in three volumes between 1830 and 1833 and is now considered a classic in geology. The theme of the first volume was Hutton's uniformitarianism, for which Lyell clearly presented substantial geological reasoning. His arguments urged scientists to explain geological phenomena by comparison with modern processes and conditions By studying modern occurrences, one could gain a better understanding of the past. He reviewed the processes of erosion, sediment accumulation, volcanic activity, and uplifting by earthquakes. Change was gradual, and even major changes in the Earth's surface structure could result from the buildup of relatively subtle changes over a sufficient period of time.

The second volume of *Principles of Geology* focused on organic evolution, that is, the change over geological time in the populations of living species, a process that Lyell considered to be fixed. Lyell stated that as former species became extinct, new distinct species emerged to maintain a continuous, natural balance. Later he altered his views on organic evolution, agreeing with Darwin that life-forms have evolved from primitive into more complex forms over time. Extinction resulted from changes in an environment's physical characteristics as well as from dynamic relationships with other species in an ecosystem. Lyell made no claims concerning the mechanism by which new species emerged.

The beginning of the third volume addressed criticisms of his first two volumes. The remainder described the application of uniformity and modern analogies to geological research and presented Lyell's classification scheme of the Tertiary formations that lay just below the most recent sedimentary deposits. (The Tertiary period occurred 65 to five million years ago.) He identified the species of embedded fossil shells, figured out how many of the species were extant, and declared the rock beds containing lower percentages of living species to be older than the ones containing more living species. This method was relative but served its purpose. He sorted the rock formations into epochs, Eocene (the oldest), Miocene, and the older and newer Pliocene (the most recent), and suggested that as time progressed, newer species replaced those driven to extinction by geological change. This volume included an appendix that contained tables of over 3,000 Tertiary fossil shells.

King's College in London appointed Lyell a professor of geology in 1831, and the general public attended his lectures in great numbers. He only held this position for two years, preferring not to have commitments outside his own research. Lyell married Mary Elizabeth Horner on July 12, 1832, and they set up a home in London. Fluent in German and French, Mary traveled with him and acted as a translator. The couple had six daughters together. As Lyell's eyes degenerated with age, she read to him and took dictation from him.

Revising and adding to his *Principles of Geology*, which went through 12 editions in his lifetime, kept Lyell busy until his death. One significant change to his 10th edition (1867–68) was the modification of the entire text to incorporate Darwin's evolutionary theory that suggested natural selection as the mechanism of action. In 1838, Lyell published an introductory geology textbook for students, *Elements of Geology*, which went through six editions. (Editions three, four, and five were titled *A Manual of Elementary Geology*.)

Expertise Abroad

In 1841, the Lyells traveled to the United States for the first time. Lyell delivered a series of lectures at the Lowell Institute in Boston and explored the geology of the Atlantic coast. He was not a polished lecturer, but his engagements were always filled to capacity with people interested in his vision of their planet in ancient times. While touring North America, he estimated the rate of recession of Niagara Falls toward Lake Erie; studied the Tertiary formations on the coasts of Virginia, the Carolinas, and Georgia; explored the Ohio Valley, Lake Erie, and Lake Ontario; examined coal in Nova Scotia; and visited an earthquake site in New Madrid, Missouri. In 1845, he published *Travels in North America*, and then returned to deliver the Lowell lectures; explore the South, including the coal fields in Alabama; investigate the growth of the *delta* of the Mississippi River; and collect fossils. After publishing *A Second Visit to the United States of North America* (1849), he returned again in 1852 and 1853.

Lyell traveled to Madeira and the Canary Islands in the Atlantic Ocean from 1853–54 to study volcanic geology. Buch had proposed the craters of elevation theory to explain the formation of volcanic islands such as Tenerife and Palma (of the Canary Islands). He thought that volcanoes were formed by the horizontal solidification of lava, followed by violent upheaval incomparable to any modern-day geological processes, and then the collapse of masses of Earth, forming tentlike roofs over large conical caverns. From his visit to France in 1828, Lyell recalled the intact cones and craters of extinct volcanoes and the unbroken sheets of lava extending from the cones in the Auvergne district. In 1859, Lyell again visited the sheets of hardened rock on the slopes of Mount Etna and Vesuvius in Italy and found no center of upheaval as would be predicted by Buch's proposed mechanism. In addition, he had seen modern lavas solidifying on 15–20-degree angled slopes on Madeira and Palma. On Etna he witnessed lavas solidifying on slopes of up to 40 degrees. In 1858, he published "On the Structure of Lavas Which Have Consolidated on Steep Slopes; With Remarks on the Mode of Origin of Mount Etna, and on the Theory of Craters of Elevation," a paper that invalidated the theory of craters of elevation.

The Age of Man

Analysis of the flora and fauna of the Canary Islands in addition to the species' geographical distribution induced Lyell to ponder the question of the origin of species. In 1856, further discussions with Darwin prepared him to accept with certainty the process of species evolution. Acceptance of the fact that species could evolve into new species forced Lyell to consider the prehistory of humans. Scientists were uncovering paleontological evidence that suggested humans had been around much longer than believed. A human skeleton with apelike features was discovered in Neanderthal, Germany, in 1857, and in 1859, a man-made tool was found embedded in ancient river gravel in France in a location previously believed to be much older than man. These developments were too important simply to add into new editions of *Elements* or *Principles*, so Lyell composed a new work, *The Geological Evidences of the Antiquity of Man*. The book summarized substantial data for the evolution, or gradual change, in all species and provided evidence that humans had evolved from other animal species over a long period of time. Though Charles Darwin had published *On the Origin of Species* in 1859, he had specifically omitted any discussion on the origin of humans, saving this discussion for the 1871 book, *The Descent of Man*. The former led to much controversial discussion concerning the evolution of humans, however, and Lyell avoided stating a clear conclusion on the matter, leaving the reader to draw his own conclusions based on the presented evidence. The blatant omission upset Darwin, who had developed a close friendship with Lyell. The following year, Lyell publicly declared his full support for Darwin's theory of indefinite modification of species by means of natural selection and completely revised the 10th edition of *Principles* to reflect this.

Knighthood and Baronetcy

Lyell's wife, Mary, died from typhoid fever in 1873, after 40 years of marriage. Lyell's own health had begun to fail in 1869. He passed away on February 22, 1875, and was buried in Westminster Abbey. Considered a classic in geology today, Lyell's *Principles of Geology* was just as popular during the 19th century, evidenced by the fact that Lyell had just finished writing the 12th edition at the time of his death. Queen Victoria conferred knighthood to Lyell in 1848 and made him a baronet in 1864. He had served as president of the

Geological Society from 1834 to 1836 and again in 1849, and president of the British Association for the Advancement of Science in 1864. The Royal Society of London awarded him both the Royal Medal (1834) and the Copley Medal (1858), and the Geological Society awarded him the Wollaston Medal (1866). At his request, the Lyell Medal was established in 1875 and is awarded annually by the Geological Society. He also made provisions for the disbursement of money from the Lyell Geological Fund to support the geological sciences.

British geologist and biographer Edward Bailey sums up Lyell's enduring contribution to the field of geology in *Charles Lyell:* "He did more than anyone else to free geology from the authority of tradition. He steadfastly sought truth through deduction from observation." *Principles of Geology* exerted a profound influence on geologists of the time by shifting the focus away from catastrophism to uniformitarianism, but Lyell affected scientists in other areas as well. Biologist Charles Darwin was heavily influenced by the idea of gradual change over time and applied it to his proposed theory of evolution by means of natural selection.

CHRONOLOGY

1797	Sir Charles Lyell is born on November 14 in Kinnordy, Kirriemuir, Scotland
1816	Enters Exeter College, Oxford University
1818	Travels with family to continental Europe. Observes the effect of moving glaciers and recognizes an age succession in rock exposures
1819	Receives a bachelor's degree in the classics from Oxford University and enters Lincoln's Inn to study law
1824	Reads his first paper, on limestone formation, to the Geological Society of London
1825–27	Practices law but continues to study geology
1830–33	Publishes the extremely successful book *Principles of Geology* in three volumes

1831–33	Works as a professor of geology at King's College in London
1834	Royal Society of London awards Lyell the Royal Medal
1845	Publishes *Travels in North America*
1848	Queen Victoria knights Lyell
1858	Publishes a paper on the structures of lava that destroys Leopold von Buch's theory of craters of elevation
1863	Publishes *The Geological Evidences of the Antiquity of Man,* about the evolution of humans
1864	Publicly declares his support for Darwin's theory of evolution by means of natural selection. Queen Victoria makes Lyell a baronet
1875	Dies on February 22 following a lengthy illness in London, England

FURTHER READING

Bailey, Edward. *Charles Lyell.* Garden City, N.Y.: Doubleday, 1963. Full-length biography written by a distinguished British geologist.

Carruthers, Margaret W., and Susan Clinton. *Pioneers of Geology: Discovering Earth's Secrets.* New York: Franklin Watts, 2001. Includes a chapter on Lyell that describes the field of geology up to Lyell's times and outlines his contributions.

Gillispie, Charles C., ed. *Dictionary of Scientific Biography.* Vol. 8. New York: Scribner, 1970–76. Good source for facts concerning personal backgrounds and scientific accomplishments but assumes reader has basic knowledge of science.

Lyell, Charles. *Principles of Geology.* Chicago: University of Chicago Press, 1990–91. A reprint of Lyell's original presentation of his uniformitarian argument.

The Unofficial Stephen Jay Gould Archive. "People: Charles Lyell." Available online. URL: http://www.stephenjaygould.org/people/charles_lyell.html. Accessed January 15, 2005. This site contains a biographical sketch and links to online versions of some of Lyell's original works and other resources.

Alfred Wegener

8

(1880–1930)

Alfred Wegener proposed the theory of continental drift, a forerunner of the theory of plate tectonics. (*Science Photo Library/Photo Researchers, Inc.*)

The Theory of Continental Drift

Even when someone is standing completely still, that person is not motionless. The Earth is rotating around the Sun and spinning on its axis, and the continents on which people live slowly but steadily drift like colossal icebergs through a sea of basalt. In 1912, a German meteorologist and polar explorer named Alfred Wegener first proposed the notion that continents have moved significant distances over hundreds of millions of years. His theory of continental displacement explained a variety of mysteries such as the uneven distribution of continents around the globe, the preferential location of mountain chains along the edges of continents, changes in climate over periods of time, earthquakes, and the geographical distribution of fossils and extant species. Early 19th-century geologists were not ready to accept Wegener's theory, later termed *continental drift*, yet decades later it revolutionized the Earth sciences.

From Astronomy to Meteorology

Alfred Lothar Wegener (pronounced VAY-geh-nehr) was born in Berlin, Germany, on November 1, 1880, to Richard and Anna Schwarz Wegener. Richard was a minister and directed a boys' orphanage. The youngest of five siblings, Alfred attended school at the Kollnisches Gymnasium and then the Universities of Heidelberg and Innsbruck. In 1905, he earned a doctorate degree in planetary astronomy from the University of Berlin, where he recalculated the Alfonsine Tables of Ptolemaic astronomy from the 13th century for his doctoral thesis. These tables were used for figuring the positions and movements of the Sun, Moon, and the planets.

Having earned an advanced degree, Wegener switched his focus to meteorology. The Royal Prussian Aeronautical Observatory near Berlin hired him to study the upper atmosphere, which he did using kites and balloons equipped with special meteorological instruments. In 1906, Wegener and his older brother Kurt broke the world record for duration of a hot air balloon flight by staying aloft for 52 hours over Germany and Denmark. After this accomplishment, a Danish expedition invited Wegener to join them as the official meteorologist in northeast Greenland from 1906 to 1908, for the purpose of studying polar air masses and glaciers. His balloon and kite skills were useful as he became the first person to study the polar atmosphere.

From 1908 to 1912, Wegener lectured on meteorology and astronomy at the Physical Institute of Marburg, in Germany. He compiled his lectures on the thermodynamics of the atmosphere into *Thermodynamik der Atmosphäre* (Thermodynamics of the atmosphere, 1911). This text became a standard in Germany and contained the foundations for the modern theory of the origin of precipitation.

A Land-Moving Theory

Wegener first considered the idea of drifting continents in 1910, when he was looking at a world atlas and was struck by the corresponding coastlines of the Atlantic Ocean. The east coast of South America and the west coast of Africa resembled giant pieces of a jigsaw puzzle that had been separated. He was not the first to notice the match, but he was the first to develop the idea that the two continents had once been joined. Wegener initially thought the idea that the continents had drifted apart was far-fetched, but the following year, while browsing through the Institute of Marburg's library, he came across paleontological evidence that supported a historical connection between the two landmasses. Other scientists had suggested that a land bridge had once spanned from Brazil to Africa but that the bridge had fallen or sunken into the ocean as the Earth cooled and contracted following its fiery genesis. Wegener did not consider this a realistic possibility, partly because the continents consist of rock that is less dense than the sea floor, but also because he could find no hard evidence to support the notion.

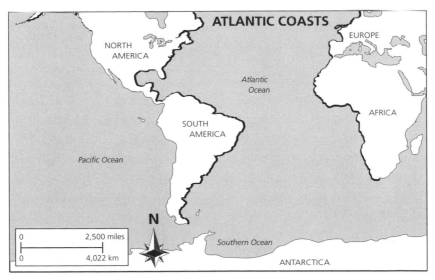

Wegener was intrigued by the complementary patterns of the coastlines of the Atlantic Ocean, particularly the fit between the east coast of South America and the west coast of Africa.

For the next year, Wegener researched paleontological, biological, and geological similarities across oceans. He found fossils for similar extinct plants and animals in both Brazil and Africa. Biological evidence, including unique species such as hippopotamuses found only in Madagascar and Africa and lemurs found only in East Africa, Madagascar, and across the Indian Ocean, indicated that those areas once must have been joined. Having discounted the land bridge theory and knowing the distance was too great for the animals to have swum or plant seeds to have been carried, Wegener considered this convincing evidence that the continents were united previously. Geologically, the composition of the Appalachian Mountains in North America resembled that of the Scottish Highlands, and the strata of the Karoo region in South Africa mirrored the strata of Santa Catarina, Brazil.

At a meeting of the Geological Association in Frankfurt on January 6, 1912, Wegener publicly presented a logical argument for his theory of continental displacement, later termed *continental drift*, in the paper, "The Geophysical Basis of the Evolution of the Large-Scale Features of the Earth's Crust (Continents and Oceans)." Four nights later, he gave a similar lecture to the Society for the Advancement of Natural Science in Marburg, Germany. The skeptical reaction from the audience of supposed experts incited Wegener to collect additional evidence for the movement of continental landmasses.

Wegener went back to Greenland from 1912 to 1913 to study glaciology and polar climatology with Danish captain J. P. Koch. The four-member team was the first to spend an entire winter on the Greenland ice cap and traverse it on foot, a 750-mile (1,207-km) distance. After returning from this second expedition, Wegener married Else Köppen, the daughter of a famous climatologist, and served as a junior officer in the German army from 1914 until 1919.

Gunshot wounds suffered during the war freed time for Wegener to develop his theory. He published his ideas in 1915, in *Die Entstehung der Kontinente und Ozeane* (*The Origin of Continents and Oceans*, 1924). The work summarized the following events: as the Permian period closed, all the landmasses were part of a single, massive continent that he called Pangaea. As the Triassic peri-

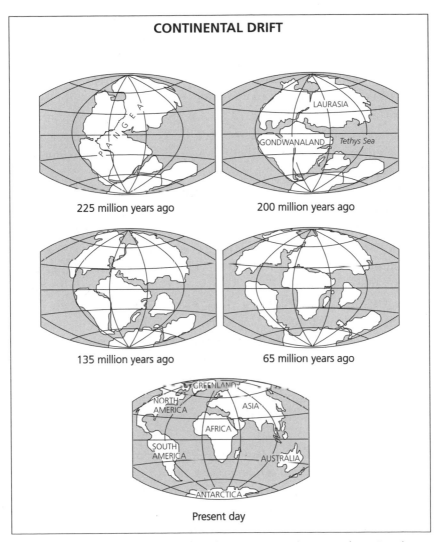

CONTINENTAL DRIFT

225 million years ago

200 million years ago

LAURASIA

GONDWANALAND   *Tethys Sea*

135 million years ago

65 million years ago

GREENLAND
NORTH
AMERICA   ASIA
AFRICA
SOUTH
AMERICA
                 AUSTRALIA
ANTARCTICA

Present day

After Wegener's death, abounding evidence supported Wegener's notion that a supercontinent, Pangaea, began splitting apart more than 200 million years ago, eventually forming the current continents.

od began, Pangaea began splitting into smaller landmasses. America broke off from Eurasia, then Africa, and it traveled westward, forming the Atlantic Ocean. India moved away from Africa (later it crashed into Asia), and Australia split from Antarctica and shifted toward the equator. Greenland split from Norway and moved north at the start of the ice ages one million years ago.

Islands were remnants of the continents plowing through the waters, and mountains formed at the front of the moving continents from the friction between the continent and the ocean floor. He hypothesized that India, Madagascar, and Africa once comprised a land called Lemuria in order to explain the distribution of lemurs and hippopotamuses. (Today scientists believe Madagascar separated from Africa about 165 million years ago.) Because marsupials currently live in Australia and the Americas, he suggested they were linked.

The theory of continental displacement fell short of a reasonable mechanical explanation for the movement of entire continents. Wegener suggested that as the planet Earth rotated from the west to the east about its axis, it created a force that caused the continents to float toward the west. He imagined the granite continents, which were less dense than the heavier basalt of the ocean floor, drifting along, plowing their way through the ocean floor, propelled by the force of the Earth's rotation. Another possible mechanism for continental movement was flight from the poles, termed *pohlflucht*, suggesting that the spinning of the Earth caused an equatorial bulge and forced material to travel toward the equator. Wegener also indicated that tidal forces played a role. Other scientists did not believe any of these forces was nearly strong enough.

After the publication of *Die Entstehung der Kontinente und Ozeane*, Wegener continued to collect data favoring continental drift. Studies in *paleoclimatology*, the study of ancient climates, strengthened his theory. For example, geographical regions that today are warm, such as South Africa, had deposits of mixed sand, gravel, boulders, and clay, indications of a melting ice sheet, signifying that it once had been much colder. The presence of fossils of plant species that typically grow in colder climates also pointed to the fact that the climates had warmed. Areas that today are frigid (such as Antarctica) contained coal, suggesting they were once tropical. As continents glided around the planet's surface, one would expect that they would experience different climates along their paths. When Wegener puzzled together a map of the continents rearranged into patterns that fit the paleoclimatological data, he found that he had reconstructed Pangaea.

A Revolution from International Controversy

As is often the case when a forward-thinking scientist puts forth a novel idea, others ignorantly ridiculed the originator. Some hesitated to take Wegener seriously because he was not a geologist by training. Others simply did not want to disrupt the basis of geological science and disregard all they had learned during the past 70 years. The accepted view was that the Earth was contracting as it cooled, and lighter rocks such as granite were rising while denser rocks such as basalt were sinking. Mountains were wrinkles that formed as the Earth contracted, and oceans were created when the crust collapsed into the shrinking core. If this were true, Wegener questioned, then why were the mountain ranges not more evenly spaced? The major factor preventing others from accepting Wegener's theory, however, was lack of a plausible mechanism.

After the war, he continued analyzing the data he collected from his Greenland expeditions and studied the origin of moon craters as the new director of the meteorological research department at the Marine Observatory in Hamburg. Because of his radical ideas, he was unable to obtain a teaching position at a German university. In 1924, Wegener moved to Austria and became a professor of meteorology and geophysics at the University of Graz.

Most scientists ignored continental drift until *paleomagnetic* science, which developed in the 1950s, renewed interest in the theory. The direction of magnetism of rocks was found to differ from the lines of magnetic force that currently existed. Advances in the field of oceanography also revealed information about the seafloor that pointed to continental movement as a real possibility.

In 1960, American marine geologists Harry Hammond Hess and Robert Sinclair Dietz independently proposed the theory of seafloor spreading, a model that provided a plausible driving force for continental movement. According to this model, the seafloor itself moves, driven by circulating currents within the Earth's mantle that bring molten rock to the surface at *mid-oceanic ridges*. As the magma rises, it spreads out and hardens, forming new floor as it forces the old seafloor out of its way. The sliding of the ocean floor carries the continents along with it.

Plate Tectonics

The most modern explanation for the movement of the continents combines portions of the continental drift and seafloor spreading models. Scientists now believe that the Earth's outer shell consists of about a dozen rigid plates that continuously glide around the globe, carrying both the ocean floor and the continents along with them. The plates glide over a layer of rock that is solid but so hot it flows. Mid-oceanic ridges mark the areas where the plates intersect.

The plates consist of a portion of the Earth's mantle, the zone in the Earth between the hard crust and the dense spherical core, and the Earth's crust, which includes all the dry land as well as the ocean floors. Because of this, the plate boundaries extend beyond the continental coastlines. The thickness of the plates ranges from five miles (8 km) to 120 miles (193 km), averaging about 60 miles (about 97 km).

Plate tectonics explains many of the Earth's surface structural characteristics. As the plates move, they interact in one of three ways. They move toward one another (forming *convergent boundaries*), away from one another (at *divergent boundaries*), or slide alongside one another (*transform plate boundaries*). Divergent boundaries create new ocean crust as magma rises up between the plates, spreads out, and solidifies. Earthquakes often occur near convergent boundaries as one plate is forced underneath another in a process called *subduction*. Earthquakes are also common near transform boundaries, also called *faults,* and volcanoes are common in subduction zones. Collisions between two convergent plates results in the formation of mountain ranges.

Scientists estimate that plates move approximately four inches (10 cm) per year, a rate that seems slow, but since they have been traveling for hundreds of millions of years, they have progressed impressive distances. Geologists believe that all the landmasses once formed a single landmass called Pangaea that broke up into two landmasses, called

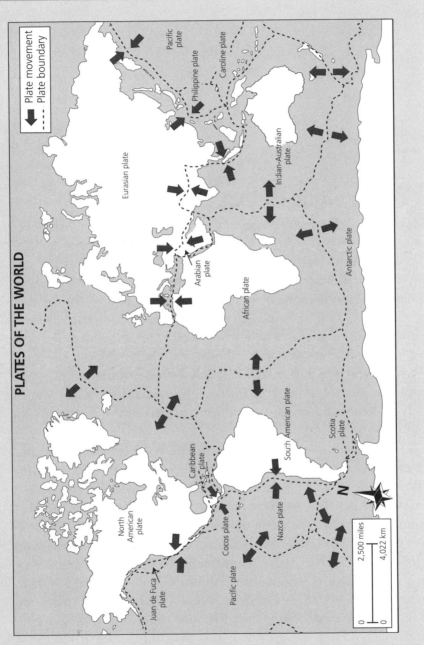

PLATES OF THE WORLD

Plate movement
Plate boundary

Pacific plate
Caroline plate
Philippine plate
Eurasian plate
Indian-Australian plate
Antarctic plate
Arabian plate
African plate
North American plate
Caribbean plate
South American plate
Scotia plate
Juan de Fuca plate
Cocos plate
Nazca plate
Pacific plate

N

2,500 miles
4,022 km
0
0

According to the theory of plate tectonics, the Earth's outer shell consists of about a dozen rigid plates that glide on a layer of hot, flowing rock.

(continues)

(continued)

Gondwanaland and *Laurasia,* about 200 million years ago. The two supercontinents eventually split into the seven major continents that exist today: North America, South America, Europe, Africa, Asia, Australia, and Antarctica.

A Bitter Cold Ending

Greenland beckoned to Wegener a third time in 1929, but the expedition had several problems, including ice storms and delays. Wegener returned a final time in spring 1930 to set up weather stations for examining the weather and atmosphere across the entire landmass in a systematic manner. On his 50th birthday, November 1st, he left a camp in central Greenland with a native after delivering some supplies and was heading west. He never arrived at his destination. Alfred Wegener's body was found during the next spring's thaw. He appeared to have suffered a heart attack while lying in his tent. His final resting place seemed fitting, so his friends built a mausoleum of ice around him and erected a 20-foot (6-m) iron cross to mark the spot.

Though he was respected as a tenacious polar explorer, Wegener never received the admiration and respect he deserved for his contributions to geology before his death. He dared to challenge the widespread belief of an unchanging Earth and threatened the prevailing notions for many geological phenomena, such as the formation of mountain ranges by wrinkling of the surface of a shrinking Earth, when he proposed that continents moved. Thirty years after his death, scientists who had the benefit of technological advancements substantiated his claims. Hess expanded and modified Wegener's theory of continental drift into seafloor spreading, which geophysicists later incorporated into the more modern theory of plate tectonics. Though Wegener was correct in purporting that continents moved, he was incorrect in believing that they plowed through the ocean floor like barges; rather, they are carried along with the ocean floor as the Earth's tectonic plates glide over a solid, yet molten, medium. Wegener's courage to persist and believe in his theory despite knowledge of an acceptable mechanism eventually revolutionized the Earth sciences.

CHRONOLOGY

1880	Alfred Lothar Wegener is born on November 1, in Berlin, Germany
1905	Obtains a doctorate in astronomy from the University of Berlin and accepts a position at the Royal Prussian Aeronautical Observatory
1906	Breaks flight record in a balloon and joins Danish expedition to Greenland to study polar air masses
1908–12	Lectures in meteorology at the Physical Institute of Marburg, in Germany
1911	Publishes *Thermodynamik der Atmosphäre* (Thermodynamics of the atmosphere)
1912	Presents theory of continental drift at the Frankfurt Geological Association meeting. His paper is titled, "The Geophysical Basis of the Evolution of the Large-Scale Features of the Earth's Crust (Continents and Oceans)"
1912–13	Leads second expedition to Greenland to study glaciology and climatology
1914–19	Serves as junior military officer for the German army during World War I
1915	Publishes theory of continental displacement in *Die Entstehung der Kontinente und Ozeane* (*The Origin of Continents and Oceans,* its English translation, is published in 1924)
1919	Works at the meteorological experimental station of the German Marine Observatory in Hamburg
1924	Becomes a professor of meteorology and geophysics at the University of Graz
1929–30	Leads third expedition to Greenland to set up weather stations

| 1930 | Leads fourth expedition to Greenland. On November 1st he leaves a base in central Greenland, heading toward a glaciological field station and is never seen alive again |
| 1931 | Expedition members find Wegener's body in May |

FURTHER READING

Adler, Robert E. *Science Firsts: From the Creation of Science to the Science of Creation.* New York: John Wiley, 2002. Stories of 35 landmark scientific discoveries, including scientific and historical contexts.

Carruthers, Margaret W., and Susan Clinton. *Pioneers of Geology: Discovering Earth's Secrets.* New York: Franklin Watts, 2001. Includes a chapter on Wegener that describes his development of the theory of continental drift.

Earth Observatory, National Aeronautics and Space Administration. "On the Shoulders of Giants: Alfred Wegener." Available online. URL: http://earthobservatory.nasa.gov/Library/Giants/Wegener. Accessed January 15, 2005. Biographical profile of Wegener with links to biographies of other scientists who have made contributions to the understanding of the Earth's climate and environmental changes.

Gillispie, Charles C., ed. *Dictionary of Scientific Biography.* Vol. 14. New York: Scribner, 1970–76. Good source for facts concerning personal backgrounds and scientific accomplishments but assumes reader has basic knowledge of science.

Horvitz, Leslie Alan. *Eureka! Scientific Breakthroughs that Changed the World.* New York: John Wiley, 2002. Explores the events and thought processes that led 12 great minds to their eureka moments.

Kious, W. Jacqueline, and Robert I. Tilling. *This Dynamic Earth: The Story of Plate Tectonics.* Available online. URL: http://pubs.usgs.gov/publications/text/dynamic.html. Last modified September 29, 2003. Originally published in book form in 1996, this site is full of information regarding plate tectonics. Follow "Historical perspective" link to find a biographical profile of Wegener and several helpful diagrams.

Arthur Holmes

(1890–1965)

Arthur Holmes dedicated his life's work to determining the true age of the Earth and developing a geological timescale. *(Science Photo Library/ Photo Researchers, Inc.)*

Estimation of the Earth's Age

Though geology as a scientific endeavor is one of the oldest natural sciences, until one man dedicated himself to dating the Earth and its geological time periods, the history of Earth was simply an ordered progression of events. Among the 20th century's most important geoscientists, Arthur Holmes was a pioneer of *geochronology* and one of the first to use radioactive evidence concealed within the rocks for determining their age. Though many scientists accepted the true age of the Earth to be 20 million years, Holmes estimated it to be closer to 4.5 billion years using methodology dependent upon the radioactive decay of unstable elements. Considered the father of geological time, Holmes was also a talented *petrologist*, and he wrote one of the field's most influential textbooks.

The 20-Million-Year Dispute

Arthur Holmes was born on January 14, 1890, in Gateshead, England, to strict Methodist parents, a cabinetmaker named David Holmes and a former schoolteacher named Emily Dickinson. Gateshead High School provided Arthur with a strong background in the sciences and an opportunity to develop his musical abilities in the Operatic Society, as Arthur was a talented pianist. He performed well at school and particularly enjoyed physics. His teacher introduced him to the age of the Earth debate that the discovery of *radioactivity* had recently refueled. In 1897 Lord Kelvin (1824–1907), a professor of natural history at Glasgow University and an eminent expert of thermodynamics, announced his newest estimation for the age of the Earth. Believing that the Earth had been gradually cooling from its molten genesis, Lord Kelvin calculated that the Earth's crust consolidated 20 million years ago, based on experimentally determined temperatures at which rocks melt and their rate of cooling. Now his long-accepted estimation was being challenged and not by geologists, who seemed to be intimidated by his stature, but by physicists.

Near the end of the 19th century, the age of the Earth was a popular topic for research and discussion among geologists, who thought the Earth was an order of magnitude older than Lord Kelvin claimed. Professor John Joly from Trinity College in Dublin supported the salinity method for estimating the age of the Earth. As the newly formed globe cooled, water condensed and formed the oceans. The water would initially be pure, but as rocks decomposed and washed over the land into the seas, the water would become saltier. Based on this assumption, if one measured the salinity of the oceans at two time points separated by a few hundred years, then one could extrapolate back to estimate how much time has passed since the water was pure, that is, when the Earth's crust solidified.

From the rate calculated for salt accumulation from erosion, Joly estimated the oceans to be over 90 million years old. One criticism for this method was that it required the rocks to lose more salt than they ever contained to supply the calculated amounts to the oceans each year. Alternatively, Irish geologist Samuel Haughton employed the simple concept that thicker strata took longer to form in order to estimate the Earth's age. After figuring that sediments accumulated on the ocean floor at a rate of one foot (30.5 cm) in 8,616 years, he estimated that it would require at least 200 million years, or possibly 10 times longer, to deposit the total thickness of rock covering the planet. Problems with this method included inaccurate estimations of the total thickness of rock on the Earth's surface and sedimentation rates that differed significantly according to time and place. Current evidence supports an increase in erosion rates over time. Even without a satisfactory means of measurement, Lord Kelvin's revised approximation of 20–40 million years appeared to be a major underestimate.

Then in 1896, French physicist Henri Becquerel discovered natural radioactivity when he observed that *uranium* emitted invisible rays of energy. Polish physicist Marie Curie studied the emanations for her doctoral dissertation and found that thorium also emitted such rays, and furthermore, the emanations were a property of atoms and not due to a chemical reaction. Curie named the revolutionary phenomenon radioactivity, and she and her husband, Pierre Curie, proceeded to discover two new radioactive elements, radium and polonium. Ernest Rutherford (1871–1937) and Frederick Soddy explained radioactivity as the result of the instability of an element that spontaneously emitted particles from its nucleus. For example, uranium released helium atoms as it decayed. In the process, an element could transform into another element. Some radioactive elements had very long *half-lives*; uranium took 4.5 billion years to decay to half of its original amount. In 1905, Rutherford suggested that radioactive decay could be used as a geological timekeeper. Using uranium/helium ratios, he determined the age of a sample of pitchblende to be 90 million years, but he incorrectly assumed that helium did not escape over time.

Pierre Curie and colleague Albert Laborde announced in 1903 that radium emitted enough heat to melt its own weight in ice in less than one hour. This finding that radioactive elements generate heat is what refueled the debate over the age of the Earth. Lord Kelvin's calculations depended on the Earth's slow cooling in an absence of any external heat source, and these physicists claimed that radioactive elements within the Earth provided enough heat to make his calculations worthless. Of course, they said it politely out of respect for the elderly and brilliant scientist, but the message was clear—the Earth may indeed be cooling, but a source of continuous heat inside the Earth rendered Lord Kelvin's thermodynamic calculations meaningless. Holmes was impressed and intrigued by these scientists who had the audacity to challenge the authoritative Lord Kelvin and by the potential utility of this phenomenon called radioactivity.

Since he was a boy, Holmes had wondered about the age of the Earth, but his parents discouraged him from questioning biblical scholars who calculated the date of creation to October 23, 4004 B.C.E. As a teenager, witnessing the debate between one of the world's most established scholars and a few lesser-known but equally smart physicists made a great impression upon Holmes. Now also interested in radioactivity, these two curiosities would merge to become his lifelong passion, using radioactive decay to determine the age of the Earth.

Entrance to the Dating Game

Holmes earned a National Scholarship Award in physics based on his outstanding higher certificate examination scores and enrolled at the Royal College of Science in London in 1907. The curriculum required all students to take mathematics, mechanics, chemistry, and physics during their first year, and Holmes took an elective geology course in his second year. The president of the Geological Society, Professor William Watts, taught the course with enthusiasm and passion, enticing Holmes to change his course of study during his third year. Fortuitously, Robert J. Strutt (1875–1947), from the Cavendish Laboratory at Cambridge University, had joined the Royal College of Science at the same time Holmes enrolled. Strutt was one of the physicists who made public his belief that radioactive elements provided a source of heat sufficient to discredit Lord Kelvin's young estimation for the age of the Earth. Strutt invited Holmes to assist him in examining helium trapped in rocks following radioactive decay. He thought that if they could measure the amount of accumulated helium and establish its rate of production, then they could calculate the age of the rock. The concept seemed simple but determining the rate of helium production was not straightforward. Because helium is a gas, an unknown but significant quantity escapes as it is produced, so the minimum age could only be estimated. (Uranium/helium measurements later were considered unreliable since the helium was not retained consistently.) After graduating from Imperial College (formerly called the Royal College of Science) in 1910, Holmes assumed this research project with Strutt as a postgraduate.

Across the ocean, American chemist Bertram Boltwood (1870–1927) recently had figured out that lead was the final product of uranium decay, and he attempted to date several rocks using uranium/lead ratios. From 26 rocks, he obtained ages ranging from 92 to 570 million years. Since helium could escape from rocks over time, he thought focusing on the end product would yield more accurate results. Unknown to chemists at the time, Boltwood's analysis was flawed due to the existence of several *isotopes* of both uranium and lead. Isotopes are forms of an element that have different atomic masses; all isotopes of an element have the same number of protons in the nucleus but differ in the number of neutrons. From his results, Boltwood constructed a rough list of geological ages.

Holmes was anxious to use radioactivity to measure the age of a rock. He carefully selected a Devonian rock from Norway that contained 17 different radioactive minerals so he could check each result against the others. After crushing the rock, extracting the minerals, and chemically separating them for analysis, he determined the ratios of uranium and lead and estimated the rock to be 370 million years old. He analyzed several others, dating the oldest at 1,640 million years, and then he proceeded to calculate ages of geological periods from measurements published by Boltwood. Holmes wrote his results, showing that as the ratio of lead to uranium increased, so did the age of the rock (since uranium decays into lead), but he wondered if some lead was already present, which would have rendered his analysis flawed.

Strutt presented Holmes's results in April 1911, at a Royal Society meeting, where fellow geologists seemed interested but were wary of the radiometric dating technique. They questioned whether it was okay to assume the uranium decay rate was constant. The complexity of the radiometric calculations confused some and intimidated others, and they had trouble accepting the possibility that the Earth was over one billion years old. Though geologists were looking for evidence indicating the Earth was older than 20 million years and knew the old techniques relied on rates of nonuniform processes, they were expecting a value closer to 100 million years, as suggested by rates of sedimentation and salt accumulation, the so-called hourglass methods.

Mozambique

In 1911, Holmes obtained a position as a geological prospector for Memba Minerals Limited. After giving his research results to Strutt, Holmes left England for Mozambique in March, beginning

Carbon Dating

Carbon dating is a technique based on the same principles of radioactive decay used by Arthur Holmes in the estimation for the age of the Earth, but it is more useful in short-range dating, with a limit of 50,000 years. Carbon-14 is a radioactive isotope of carbon-12 and has a half-life of 5,730 years, short in comparison to other radioactive isotopes. Carbon-14 is also unique because it is created continuously in the Earth's upper atmosphere by the collision of neutrons from cosmic rays with nitrogen-14 atoms and the accompanying release of a proton. Newly created carbon-14 oxidizes to carbon dioxide (CO_2) almost immediately. In the biosphere, photosynthetic organisms such as green plants and plankton

a physically difficult and emotionally stressful six-month expedition in search of economically valuable minerals.

While there, Holmes contracted malaria, and high fevers occasionally forced him to rest for several days. Lying in bed, he could not stop thinking about radiometric dating and contemplated how he could reconcile data obtained by radiometric methods with data calculated from sedimentation rates. Without access to geology textbooks or journals, he used his memory to approximate the amount of original igneous rocks from which sediments had been derived, then figured out how long it would have taken for the sediments to be deposited. His estimate was 325 million years since the base of the Cambrian period, not too far from the value of 500 million years that he obtained using radiometric methods. He wrote a friend asking him to publish his results.

Though prospecting for precious minerals was unsuccessful in Mozambique, during the trip, Holmes developed a lifelong interest in Precambrian time and a new commitment to constructing a geological timescale. He collected zircons, minerals good for age

uptake the radioactive CO_2 and incorporate the carbon-14 into organic molecules that journey up the food chain.

In the late 1940s, Willard Frank Libby (1908–80) and his colleagues at the University of Chicago recognized the advantages that incorporation of this isotope into living organisms provided for dating organic matter, including substances such as coal, bones, and wood. Approximately one of every trillion carbon atoms that comprise a living organism is the carbon-14 isotope. After death, an organism no longer takes in radioactive carbon-14, but the already present carbon-14 continues to decay, so its concentration decreases over time in comparison with atmospheric levels. Calculations performed from measurements of residual radioactivity of a sample reveal the date of death. Libby received the Nobel Prize in chemistry in 1960 for developing this method using carbon-14 for age determinations in archaeology, geology, and other branches of science.

determinations, and several samples of never-examined Precambrian rock types. As the prospectors headed back home, Holmes became gravely ill with black water fever. The nuns at the hospital in Mozambique prematurely telegraphed news of his death to London, but Holmes miraculously recovered and arrived back in Southampton in November 1911. He continued to suffer from bouts of malaria for years afterward.

The Problem with Lead

In 1912, Imperial College offered Holmes a position as a demonstrator in geology, and in July 1914, the 23-year-old geologist married Margaret Howe. The newlyweds moved to Chelsea, and Holmes kept busy lecturing and researching the petrographical material he brought back from Mozambique. When World War I broke out in August, the military declared Holmes unfit for military service due to his recurring bouts of malaria. His contributions toward the war effort included making scaled topography maps for naval intelligence and researching alternative sources of potash, an ingredient of fertilizer formerly supplied to Great Britain by Germany. With much of Imperial's faculty, staff, and student body on leave serving in the war, Holmes had plenty of time to delve into his studies.

In an attempt to convince his contemporaries of the usefulness of radiometric dating, he composed *The Age of the Earth* (1913), a review of the historical methods for estimating ages of geological materials, that also presented all the current related evidence and contrasted the results obtained by different techniques. He pointed out problems with the other approaches and defended his own estimation of 1,600 million years based on uranium/lead measurements. The book was highly successful, but the more established geologists continued to question the legitimacy of his technique.

The possibility that some "ordinary" lead, around since the formation of the Earth, was already present in the rock samples before any radioactive decaying took place was troublesome. Another difficulty in using lead measurements was that in addition to uranium, the radioactive element thorium also decayed to lead. To overcome this, Bob Lawson, a friend from childhood who worked at the Radium Institute of Vienna, determined the atomic masses of the three lead isotopes, enabling one to adjust age calculations accordingly based on the proportions of each type.

Holmes thought he resolved a means to determine the age of rocks with accuracy, but he did not know yet that uranium also had another isotope. Uranium-238 comprises 99 percent of the total uranium, but uranium-235 decays at a faster rate, and Holmes unknowingly included its end product as part of the ordinary lead. This isotope hitch prevented some skeptics from recognizing the promise of this new dating technique.

Misfortune and Providence

By the end of World War I, Holmes had written three books but was still only a demonstrator at Imperial College. In 1918, Maggie and Arthur had welcomed their first child, Norman, and a meager demonstrator's income was not sufficient to support the family. The Yomah Oil Company hired Holmes as chief geologist with the promise of a much larger salary. His family moved to Burma in November 1920 and settled in Yenangyaung, where Holmes spent two years frantically searching for new oil finds to save the struggling company. Loyalty to the company kept him working long after the then-bankrupt company stopped paying him, and before they finally returned to England in late 1922, their beloved son Norman died from severe dysentery, devastating Holmes. The job that Holmes hoped would benefit his family left them penniless, and he had to sue to try to recover his salary.

Without an institutional affiliation, Holmes could not secure funding to continue his research. For a while, Holmes worked in a fur, brass goods, and knick-knack shop that he opened with Maggie's cousin. His marriage was deteriorating, but soon Maggie was pregnant with their second son, born in February 1924. The year Geoffrey was born, the University of Durham happened to be improving and expanding their science programs. They needed a reader for geology, and Holmes gratefully accepted the offered position. The following year he became head of the geology department, of which he was the only faculty member. He was a popular lecturer, and the few students who came through the geology department each year thought he was a fair teacher and a caring mentor.

The Powerful Engine of Radioactivity

While Holmes's major passion was finding absolutes for geological time, he was also knowledgeable about other subjects. In 1915, German meteorologist Alfred Wegener (1880–1930) proposed the theory of continental drift, suggesting all the continents once were part of an enormous supercontinent that broke into pieces that have been drifting around the globe for millions of years. This model was exciting because it explained many unusual geological (and biological and climatological) phenomena, but most geologists hesitated to accept it without a plausible mechanism. The English translation of Wegener's book *The Origin of the Continents and Oceans* in 1924 aroused a heated debate, and Holmes was among the few geologists who were progressive enough to entertain the idea.

Aware of the enormous energy provided by radioactivity, Holmes believed that the intense heat generated by the radioactive decay of unstable elements within the Earth's interior was a sufficiently powerful engine for moving continents. The substratum, or mantle, was solid, but he thought that over millions of years it behaved like a thick liquid. Holmes proposed thermal convection as a means to dissipate the heat, causing the cooler material close to the surface to sink, leaving space for hotter, less dense material to rise and fill. In December 1929, Holmes proposed to the Geological Society of Glasgow that convection currents were responsible for continental drift. He explained that as convection currents in the mantle cooled and descended, they could drag continents horizontally across the Earth's surface. "Radioactivity and Earth Movements," his seminal paper, was published in the *Transactions of the Geological Society of Glasgow* in 1931. Though Holmes had a respectable scientific reputation, his ideas were mostly ignored until the 1960s, when American geophysicists Harry Hammond Hess and Robert Sinclair Dietz independently proposed the concept of seafloor spreading, which in combination with continental drift has evolved into the well-supported theory of plate tectonics.

Holmes traveled to give invited lectures around the world, including in the United States in 1932. He took advantage of this opportunity to solicit help in constructing a geological timescale from American scientists, who seemed to have more money and time available for research than did the British. His demanding schedule forced Durham to hire another lecturer in the geology department in 1933; they selected Doris L. Reynolds, a notable petrologist with whom Holmes had been having an affair since 1931. In 1938, Maggie died from stomach cancer, and Holmes married Reynolds in 1939.

A Fourth Isotope

Since his days in Mozambique, Holmes wanted to develop a geological timescale with dates defining the beginning of each period and epoch. The work of previous geologists allowed for the construction of a geological column organized by characteristics of the layers of rock and by the distinctive fossils contained within the strata. These historical determiners permitted relative ordering but not the assignment of specific dates for the time periods. Holmes needed a framework on which to build and asked chemistry professor Fritz Paneth in Berlin for assistance. In 1928, Paneth developed a precise assay for measuring very small amounts of helium and used it to analyze two famous rocks from known geological periods: the Whin Sill from the late Carboniferous period and the Cleveland Dyke from the middle to early Tertiary period. Paneth dated the Whin Sill at 182 million years and the Cleveland Dyke at 26 million years, ages that seemed to agree with the geological evidence. (Today the Whin Sill and Cleveland Dyke are believed to be approximately 295 and 60 million years, respectively.) These two rocks did not have enough lead to determine lead ages as controls, but Holmes was anxious to make progress and confident that a geological timescale was possible.

Geologists were now more accepting of the longer estimates for the age of the Earth, which Holmes reported in his second edition of *The Age of the Earth* (1927) to be between 1,600 and 3,000 million years based on the uranium and lead measurements. The book also contained a geological scale based on lead ratios and helium ratios, but two decades brought little progress—Holmes was able to summarize all the computed mineral ages in a single short table.

The invention of the first mass spectrograph by English chemist Francis William Aston enabled the identification of isotopes with different atomic weights. Aston used his mass spectrograph to discover no less than 212 naturally occurring isotopes and was awarded the Nobel Prize in chemistry for 1922. The mass spectrograph evolved into the more advanced modern mass spectrometer that separates isotopes by passing them through a magnetic field that deflects them to different degrees based on their mass and the charge of the field. In the late 1920s, Aston clearly identified three known lead isotopes, a finding with major implications for radioactive dating. He also unexpectedly noted that the isotope believed to be ordinary lead was in fact an end product from the decay of another less abundant uranium isotope that Rutherford helped identify as uranium-235. Rutherford estimated the uranium-235 decay rate, assumed that at the time of the Earth's formation uranium-235 and uranium-238 were present in equal amounts, and calculated the length of time it would have taken for the equal amounts of the two isotopes to decay to their current ratios. He obtained an astounding value of 3,400 million years, but his results and similar results from a few other geologists were mostly ignored.

If uranium-235 decayed to lead-207, then did so-called ordinary lead exist at all? In 1937, a physicist from Harvard University, Alfred Nier, began exploring the questionable existence of ordinary lead using a new mass spectrometer that had been treated with fastidious care to ensure no contaminating lead was present. He easily identified the three known lead isotopes, but he also observed a tiny amount of a fourth lead isotope with an atomic mass of 204 that was not produced by radioactive decay.

Primeval Lead Composition

By the 1940s, geologists had accepted the billion-year range for the age of the Earth, but no one had assigned absolute times to the geological timescale. One problem was that accurate ages could only be obtained from igneous rocks, since they contained high amounts of lead, but it was hard to know their geological age. Nier surmised that since two isotopes of uranium decayed to lead (uranium-238 decayed to lead-206 with a half-life of 4.5 billion years, and uranium-235 decayed to lead-207 with a half-life of 700

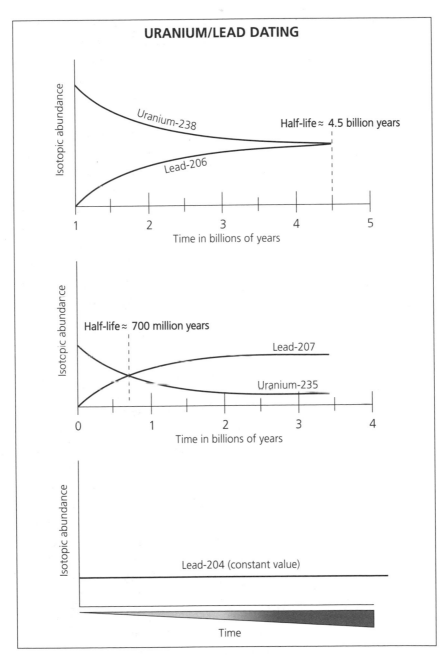

URANIUM/LEAD DATING

Isotopic abundance

Uranium-238

Half-life ≈ 4.5 billion years

Lead-206

1   2   3   4   5
Time in billions of years

Isotopic abundance

Half-life ≈ 700 million years

Lead-207

Uranium-235

0   1   2   3   4
Time in billions of years

Isotopic abundance

Lead-204 (constant value)

Time

Because two different isotopes of uranium decay to two different isotopes
of lead and the amount of ordinary lead remains constant, dating with these
elements provides an inherent means for triple checking results.

million years), comparison of both lead isotope growth rates to the constant value of the fourth isotope, lead-204, would reveal an accurate age. To test the validity of this lead-lead method, he dated 25 ancient lead ores with very low lead ratios and found the calculated ages from the different "clocks" generally agreed.

Holmes decided to employ a novel approach for determining an accurate age of the Earth that he had considered years before. His method was dependent on primeval isotope ratios, the ratios present during the Earth's genesis. Since uranium and thorium were formed, they have been decaying continually, while the amount of ordinary lead has remained stable. Since the primeval lead composition would have been trapped and fossilized inside minerals as the newly formed crust solidified, one should be able to locate minerals with ancient parts of the Earth's crust from which the primeval composition of lead could be identified. Then one could calculate the time elapsed since the Earth's primeval mix of lead isotopes began to be contaminated by radiogenic lead. With the assistance of a newly acquired Marchant calculating machine, Holmes used this method to confidently calculate the age of a rock sample from an ancient galena (lead ore) from Greenland to be three billion years old. Holmes rightly felt this was a defining moment in his efforts to age the Earth.

Under the assumption that the galena represented primeval lead, Holmes used Nier's measurements to calculate over 1,400 solutions for the age of the Earth. When he plotted the frequencies of each computed age, he obtained a well-defined peak at 3,350 million years. Though the rock samples that he used did not contain the primeval lead values, the mathematical approach he developed formed the basis of the one used today. Because a German named Fiesel Houtermans used a similar technique, the method is referred to as the Holmes-Houtermans model for dating the Earth. By this time in 1946, geologists accepted isotope dating but still debated the best means for applying its use.

Next Holmes constructed a geological timescale that reconciled his new radiometric results with the hourglass estimations. He began by collecting information on sediment thicknesses from around the world, and then plotted the thicknesses to scale for the whole geological column from the present day to the base of the Cambrian period. He incorporated dates calculated from Nier's

1947 GEOLOGICAL TIME SCALE

Base ages in millions of years

Geological stage	Determined by Holmes	Currently accepted
Pleistocene Epoch	1	1.8
Pliocene Epoch	12	5.3
Miocene Epoch	26	24
Oligocene Epoch	38	34
Eocene Epoch	58	56
Paleocene Epoch	—	65
Cretaceous Period	127	145
Jurassic Period	152	213
Triassic Period	182	248
Permian Period	203	286
Carboniferous Period	255	360
Devonian Period	313	410
Silurian Period	350	440
Ordovician Period	430	505
Cambrian Period	510	544

Holmes assigned years to geological periods based on a combination of sedimentation data and radiometric calculations.

data by using primeval lead ratios, plotted the five most probable ages as control points, and extrapolated to estimate dates for the bases of other geological periods. He published his results, "The Construction of a Geological Time Scale," in *Transactions of the Geological Society of Glasgow* in 1947, aware of the fact that accumulation rates were not constant. He frequently adjusted his scale to accommodate corrected information and include additional data obtained by new techniques, and in 1959 he published "A Revised Geological Time Scale" in *Transactions*. In 1953 Clair Patterson and Harrison Brown obtained very accurate primeval lead isotope measurements from an iron meteorite formed at the same time as the Earth and computed the value of 4.55 billion years for the age of the Earth. Though in the last 50 years scientists have obtained new data and made adjustments to improve accuracy, the assessment of 4.55 billion years remains the currently accepted value.

The End of Time for a Famous Geologist

Having accomplished his two career goals of dating the Earth and constructing a geological timescale that could be applied to common rocks, Holmes concentrated on his duties as a professor. In 1943, the University of Edinburgh had appointed him regius professor of geology, a position subsidized by the king himself. The outbreak of World War II forced Holmes to reduce the length of his geology course from one year to six months. Though it would have saved lecture time to assign the students reading material before coming to class, no geology textbook contained information about the recent developments in the field, such as radiometric dating and continental drift. Holmes took it upon himself to compose a book based on his lecture notes. When he published *Principles of Physical Geology* in 1944, it became an immediate best seller and was reprinted over 18 times during the following 20 years. The success of the book was largely due to his ability to write for the average reader and clearly present the major questions of physical geology.

Holmes became ill in 1948 and lost all of his energy and interest in work. The doctor ordered complete rest, and he and his wife spent the summer in Ireland. After recovering, Holmes focused on Precambrian geology and revised Africa's geological map based on radiometric dates. His heart began to deteriorate, and in 1956, he retired from the University of Edinburgh.

The distinguished geologist belonged to numerous scientific organizations and received many honors and awards during his career. The Geological Society of London gave Holmes their Murchison Medal in 1940 and their highest award, the Wollaston Medal, in 1956. The Geological Society of America awarded Holmes their Penrose Medal in 1956 for his outstanding contributions in the science of geology. In 1964, Holmes received the Vetlesen Prize, the greatest honor for a geologist, for his "uniquely distinguished achievement in the sciences resulting in a clearer understanding of the Earth, its history, and its relation to the universe." His health was too frail to travel to Columbia University for the award ceremony, but he did find the strength to tackle one more major project, revising *Principles of Physical Geology*. He finished just a few months before he died of bronchial pneumonia on September 20, 1965, in London.

Arthur Holmes was a quiet man but did not avoid the controversial topics of geology in his day; in particular, the antiquity of the Earth and continental drift. His background in physics convinced him radiometric dating was the most accurate means for determining the age of rocks and the Earth, making him the right man for the job of providing actual ages for Earth's geological episodes. The implications of Holmes's estimate for an ancient Earth were widespread; they forced astronomers to reexamine the age of the universe and gave biologists reasonable time to allow for the occurrence of evolutionary processes. Though his contributions toward advancing the idea of drifting continents are often overlooked, Holmes was the first to propose convection currents as a plausible moving force. Today scientists believe the Earth formed 4.5 billion years ago because the father of geological time had a passion for seeking the truth and dedicated himself to laying the groundwork for using the natural geological clocks within the rocks.

CHRONOLOGY

1890	Arthur Holmes is born on January 14 in Gateshead, England.
1910	Graduates in geology and physics from Imperial College in London and begins studying radioactivity in rocks with R. J. Strutt
1911	Labors as a geological prospector in Mozambique. Strutt presents Holmes's radiometric dating results of a Devonian rock to the Royal Society
1912–20	Works as demonstrator in geology at Imperial College
1913	Uses phenomenon of radioactivity to estimate the age of the Earth at 1,600 million years and publishes the first edition of *The Age of the Earth*
1920–22	Works as chief geologist for an oil company in Burma

1924	Becomes reader in geology at the University of Durham
1925–43	Heads geology department at the University of Durham
1927	Publishes second edition of *The Age of the Earth,* including a geological timescale
1929	Proposes convection currents as a mechanism for continental drift at a meeting of the Geological Society of Glasgow
1931	Publishes "Radioactivity and Earth Movements"
1943	Becomes regius professor of geology at the University of Edinburgh
1944	Publishes first edition of the classic textbook *Principles of Physical Geology*
1947	Constructs geological timescale obtained by combining sedimentation thicknesses with radiometric data
1956	Retires from the University of Edinburgh due to declining health
1959	Publishes revised geological timescale
1965	Having completed major revisions for the second edition of *Principles of Physical Geology,* Holmes dies on September 20 in London, at age 75, from bronchial pneumonia

FURTHER READING

Biographical Memoirs of Fellows of the Royal Society of London. Vol. 12. London: The Royal Society, 1966. Authoritative, full memoir written by a distinguished colleague.

Encyclopedia of World Biography. Vol. 7, 2nd ed. Farmington Hills, Mich.: Thomson Gale, 1998. Brief biographies of notable figures and summaries of their accomplishments, written for high school students.

Geologic Time: Online Edition. Available online. URL: http://pubs. usgs.gov/gip/geotime. Last updated December 11, 2000. Summarizes concepts, historical information, and techniques relating to geological time, relative and radiometric timescales, and the age of the Earth.

Gillispie, Charles C., ed. *Dictionary of Scientific Biography*. Vol. 6. New York: Scribner, 1970–76. Good source for facts concerning personal backgrounds and scientific accomplishments but assumes reader has basic knowledge of science.

Lewis, Cherry. *The Dating Game: One Man's Search for the Age of the Earth*. New York: Cambridge University Press, 2000. Detailed account of Holmes's lifelong pursuits to determine the age of the Earth and develop a geological timescale.

Stephen Jay Gould

(1941-2002)

Stephen Jay Gould was a prominent 20th-century paleontologist most famous for proposing the theory of punctuated equilibrium. *(Courtesy of Justin Ide, Harvard University News Office)*

Theory of Punctuated Equilibrium

Through the study of fossils, paleontologists can learn about the unique life-forms that existed during different geological periods. Geologists use fossil species to estimate the age of the rocks in which they are embedded and also to gain information about the Earth's physical environment during those times. Over the past few decades, one major area of research in *paleobiology*, the subdiscipline of paleontology that focuses on the floral and faunal fossil species, has been the processes that cause the large-scale evolutionary changes documented in the fossil record. As the original expounder of the theory of evolution by natural selection, Charles Darwin (1809–82) is the most famous evolutionary biologist. He proposed that organisms with reproductively advantageous modifications passed on the favorable characteristics to their offspring and that the accumulation of these slight variations led to the eventual development of new species. These concepts still form the basis of modern evolutionary thought, but the proposal of *punctuated equilibrium* by Stephen Jay Gould and Niles Eldredge (1942–   ) in 1972 significantly modified the original model of natural selection. Trained in paleontology, Gould was the 20th century's most prominent interpreter of evolutionary thought. He was a prolific, award-winning author, particularly concerning the origins and diversity of life, who wrote for the general public as well as for a scientific audience.

A Young Boy's Interest in Paleontology

Stephen Jay Gould was born on September 10, 1941, in New York City. Steve was the older of two sons born to Eleanor Rosenberg Gould and Leonard Gould, a court stenographer who enjoyed natural history. At the age of five, Steve resolved to become a paleontologist after seeing the *Tyrannosaurus rex* exhibit at the American Museum of Natural History in Manhattan. When he was 11 years old, he read *The Meaning of Evolution* (1949), written by the curator of the department of geology and paleontology at the American Museum of Natural History, George Gaylord Simpson, who helped establish the modern synthesis of Darwin's theory of evolution by natural selection. Though he only minimally understood what he read, he was fascinated by it. His high school did not provide adequate instruction on evolution, so Steve began reading Darwin's work independently. He would later unite his two interests of paleontology and evolution.

Steve spent the summer after high school at the University of Colorado and then enrolled at Antioch College in Yellow Springs, Ohio. The intellectual and creative genius of evolutionist Charles Darwin impressed Gould, though he would later challenge his description of the progression of evolution. He completed his bachelor's degree with a double major in geology and philosophy in 1963. At Columbia University, Gould pursued a doctorate degree in evolutionary biology and paleontology by researching fossil land snails in Bermuda. To trace the evolutionary history of the snails, he searched strata representing millions of years but found basically no changes. A fellow graduate student and future collaborator, Niles Eldredge, observed a similar phenomenon in trilobites.

In 1965, Gould married an artist named Deborah Lee, with whom he had two sons, and accepted a position as an assistant professor of geology at Antioch in 1966. The following year he completed his doctorate in paleontology and became an assistant professor of geology and assistant curator of invertebrate paleontology for the Museum of Comparative Zoology at Harvard University, where he continued researching the evolution of snails. He remained at Harvard for his entire life, becoming an associate professor in 1971 and a full professor only two years afterward. In 1982, he was named the Alexander Agassiz Professor of Zoology.

Evolution by Jerks

As an undergraduate student of geology, Gould dared to question the constancy inherent in uniformitarianism, the principle that asserts the Earth's physical features result from geological processes that have operated steadily and in the same manner since its formation 4.5 billion years ago. Why assume rates were constant and unchanging? He wrote a paper titled "Hume and Uniformitarianism" that examined the assumption of constancy of natural laws in order to reach scientific conclusions about the past. He published a revised version, "Is Uniformitarianism Necessary?" in the *American Journal of Science* in 1965. Gould continued thinking about uniformitarianism and the other extreme, catastrophism, the belief that Earth's geological formations, such as mountains and lakes, resulted from tremendous catastrophes, such as floods or earthquakes. Years later, he described the concepts of time and direction in geology in the technical book *Time's Arrow, Time's Cycle* (1987).

Darwin's View

One of the most influential books of all time, Charles Darwin's *On the Origin of Species by Means of Natural Selection,* embodied two major themes, descent with modification and natural selection, both of which are indelibly associated with his name. Today the term *evolution* connotes a variety of meanings, but in his original text Darwin did not use the word *evolution* until the very end. He described the process of change as descent with modification. Natural selection was the mechanism for adaptive evolutionary change that resulted in the establishment of characteristics that increased the reproductive success of organisms. The premise of Darwinian evolution was that the accumulation of numerous variations over time resulted in the creation of new species.

Darwin pictured the history of life to be like a family tree, with the trunk representing the oldest ancestors, to which everyone was related, and the end of each branch representing a distinct species, or individual

Gould supported evolutionary theory, but without convincing evidence for slow, gradual transitions between species, he questioned the widely accepted manner by which it occurred. *Phyletic gradualism,* rooted in Darwinism but slightly modified, maintained that speciation occurred from the slow and steady transformation of entire populations over a large geographic range, but data indicated that evolution occurred in sudden, rapid spurts followed by longer periods with no substantial changes. Eldredge and Gould published "Punctuated Equilibria: An Alternative to Phyletic Gradualism" in *Models in Paleobiology* in 1972. This paper attempted to explain the tempo and pattern of evolution by fossil evidence and helped revitalize paleontology by generating a vast amount of literature in response. The paper also contained a warning to scientists about the danger of seeing only what an accepted theory dic-

family members. Physical proximity between species on the imagined tree revealed the closeness of the relationship between two distinct species. On the tree of life, the points where new branches emerged denoted ancestral organisms evolving into new species, just as branching on a family tree signifies the birth of a new family member. The branches themselves represented the accumulation of many modifications that over millions of years might eventually prohibit descendents of a common ancestor from being able to sexually reproduce with each other, creating new biological species.

Darwin anticipated the major criticism for his proposal of gradual *speciation* by the accumulation of variations over time to be the absence of transitional forms in the fossil record. If speciation were a continuous process, then paleontologists should be able to document the progressive development of modern species from their ancestral forms; however, examination of fossil species did not support gradual modification. Darwin referred to the absence of intermediate fossil species as "imperfections in the fossil record" caused by decomposition, metamorphism, deposition, and tectonism. He suggested that over time, paleontologists would find the missing fossils and fill in the gaps within lineages.

tated and suggested that paleontological research and comprehension of the Earth's true history had been hindered by the assumption of phyletic gradualism.

Gould was disappointed in Darwin for attributing the absence of nongradualistic fossil evidence to imperfections in the fossil record. He also noticed that some variations did not provide adaptive improvements and therefore could not be explained by Darwinian logic. Eldredge and Gould proposed that the abrupt appearance and stasis of species in the stratigraphical record was consistent with *allopatric speciation*, speciation occurring in small geographically separated subpopulations. Within a large population, new genetic variations became lost within an even larger mix of forms for a specific characteristic, but if an individual that carried the genetic variation was isolated from the rest of the population so that gene flow is

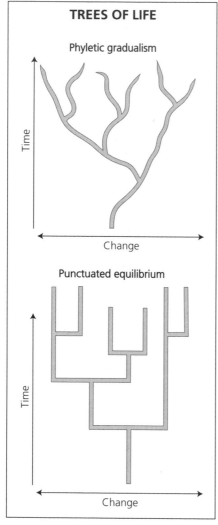

TREES OF LIFE

Phyletic gradualism

Time

Change

Punctuated equilibrium

Time

Change

The upper diagram represents phyletic gradualism, in which slight variations accumulate over long periods of time, eventually leading to the creation of new species. The lower diagram represents punctuated equilibrium, in which speciation occurs rapidly (geologically speaking) and is followed by long periods of essentially no change.

reduced, then that variation has a greater chance of becoming established in a separated subpopulation, resulting in lineage splitting. One would expect transitional fossils to be rare if speciation occurred abruptly in small peripheral populations.

Eldredge and Gould believed that the breaks in the fossil record accurately depicted the past. New species did not evolve within the same geographic area, and entire populations did not gradually transform into new species. In contrast, they proposed that speciation was a rapid event that occurred in a small isolated population, followed by a long period of stasis, with no change, a model called punctuated equilibrium (PE).

Reactions to PE varied. Some paleontologists felt the need to defend gradualism and flaunted the few well-documented examples. One classic example in paleontology is the slow, progressive increase in the number of whorls in the Liassic oyster *Gryphaea*. Biologists were surprised at the abundant evidence demonstrating that species remain virtually unchanged for millions of years, even in the face of rapid geological or climatological change. Organisms appeared to migrate rather than adapt to sudden climactic shifts. Critics of PE labeled it "evolution by jerks." Gould wittingly responded by calling gradualism "evolution by creeps."

Though the title of the original paper introducing PE called it an alternative to Darwin's gradualism, Gould later explained that the two methods did not operate exclusively. Examinations of the overall fossil fauna overwhelmingly supported PE, whereas support for gradualism usually was found by investigating a specific lineage. PE explained why intermediate fossils connecting related species were absent; however, transitional fossils between major lineages did exist.

Gould published several follow-up papers expanding the theory of PE. While some criticized his ideas, saying he made PE out to be more important than it actually was or that periods of stasis were simply a lame attempt to explain missing links in the fossil record, others recognized his work as brilliant. The Paleontological Society awarded him the Schuchert Award in 1975 for excellence in paleontological research by a scientist less than 40 years of age.

A Prolific and Influential Writer

In addition to more than 1,000 scientific papers, Gould authored at least 20 books, interestingly, all using a manual typewriter. Between 1974 and 2001, Gould published a series of 300 consecutive monthly essays for a column titled "This View of Life" in the magazine *Natural History*. His enlightening discourses ranged in scope over topics of science, philosophy, history, art, and literature and were collected and republished in 10 volumes under intriguing titles such as *Hen's Teeth and Horse's Toes* (1983) and *I Have Landed* (2002). Readers appreciated his ability to explain complex topics such as evolution and other natural phenomena without oversimplifying them. *The Panda's Thumb* (1980), a book that described a wrist bone that pandas use to help them strip bark from bamboo shoots and allowed them to switch from eating meat to eating plants, received the 1981 American Book Award in science. The following year Gould won the National Book Critics Circle Award for his book *The Mismeasure of Man*, which attacked the misuse of standardized intelligence tests to discriminate against certain races and religions. His *Wonderful Life: The Burgess Shale and the Nature of History* (1989) won the Rhône-Poulenc Prize, a literary award for the best nonfiction science book written for the general reader. The best seller described a British Columbia limestone quarry that formed 530 million years ago and holds a variety of unusual and complex fossil remains. Gould used this geological structure as an illustration of the characteristic randomness of evolution. He believed that evolution did not purposefully strive toward perfection and encouraged people to wonder "what if" biological history had proceeded down a different path.

Because of his recognized expertise on evolution and his ability to communicate scientific concepts lucidly, Gould served as a witness in an Arkansas state trial challenging the teaching in public schools of so-called creation science alongside evolution. Gould demonstrated that *intelligent design*, the belief that a higher being created the Earth, had no scientific basis, and that in fact, scientific evidence discredited many biblical stories that creationists interpreted as literal truths. The court ruled in favor of eliminating creationist teaching from the curriculum on the basis that it was religion and did not meet the criteria to qualify as science.

A New Structure for Evolutionary Theory

Gould's last contribution to scientific libraries was a mammoth 1,433-page treatise, *The Structure of Evolutionary Theory*, written over two decades and published in 2002. In the book, he reviewed the undeniable facts of Darwinian evolution: more offspring are produced than can survive given competition for resources within a population, variations occur within individuals, and the variations are passed on to the next generation. Natural selection provided the mechanism by which variants that were better adapted to a particular environment achieved better reproductive success and passed on the favorable characteristics to their offspring. A master of analogy, Gould compared the framework of Darwin's evolutionary theory to a piece of coral with three major limbs branching from a central

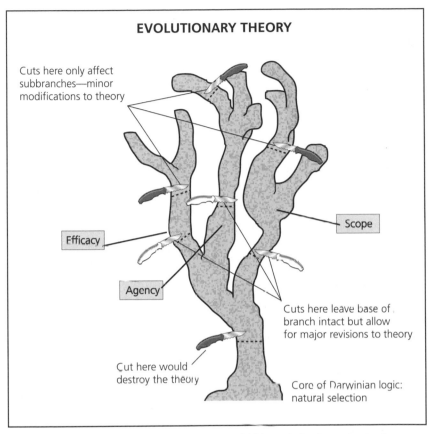

EVOLUTIONARY THEORY

Cuts here only affect subbranches—minor modifications to theory

Scope

Efficacy

Agency

Cuts here leave base of branch intact but allow for major revisions to theory

Cut here would destroy the theory

Core of Darwinian logic: natural selection

In *The Structure of Evolutionary Theory,* Gould likened the framework of evolution to a coral, with three branches representing the tripod of Darwinian logic: agency, efficacy, and scope.

trunk. The trunk represented the core of Darwinian logic, the theory of natural selection, and the three branches represented a tripod of agency, efficacy, and scope. The central branch represented the agency by which natural selection worked—the claim that natural selection worked on organisms, not genes or *clades* or any other level in the hierarchical organization of life. The second branch represented the efficacy of natural selection—that natural selection alone was the mechanism for adaptive evolutionary change. The third branch symbolized the scope of natural selection, the extrapolation that small microevolutionary variations such as those that transformed wolves into dogs, explained all taxonomic diversity given the immensity of geological time. Gould explained that severing the central trunk or disproving natural selection as an evolutionary force would destroy the theory (as it would kill the organism). Severing close to the branch points of the three major limbs would significantly compromise the theory, but excising and regrafting other parts would maintain the essential nature of the theory.

Gould proceeded to expand, add, and redefine aspects of classical evolution to restructure the symbolic coral, allowing growth of stronger branches to occur. The accumulation of new and different types of data over the 30 years since Eldredge and Gould first proposed PE allowed Gould to revise the structure of evolutionary theory by regrafting upon the original foundation. The recognition of species as Darwinian individuals capable of participating in natural selection led to a generalization of the hierarchical theory and the expansion of the agency branch by permitting selection to act on multiple levels in the hierarchy of life: genes, cells, organisms, demes, species, and clades. Gould cut back the efficacy branch a little, maintaining that creativity was necessary to build "evolutionary novelties" but allowing for a variety of additional mechanisms to guide evolutionary pathways by imposing some constraints (such as structural or developmental). For example, as the diameter of a single-celled organism increases, the ratio of its surface area to its volume exponentially decreases. Physical forces limit the maximum size of a cell since the surface area of the membrane of a very large cell could not support the required amount of material exchange with the environment. Gould did not feel microevolutionary processes were sufficient to explain the extent of diversity of life despite the vastness of geological time, so he modified the scope branch to include the role of broader scale operations in the establishment of new species. The discovery of a catastrophic mass extinction occurring 65 million years ago supported this modification to evolutionary theory. Scientists found an unusually high level of iridium, an element found in meteors, comets, and the Earth's mantle, within a layer of sediment deposited around that time, suggesting an extraterrestrial impact and the resulting environmental disturbances caused the extinction of 85 percent of all species at the end of the Cretaceous period.

Reflections and Miscellany

Gould exhibited an extraordinary breadth of knowledge, and people often asked his opinions on divisive issues. Though frequently questioned about the possibility of life on other planets, he never responded with a simple yes or no but took care to explain that, given the variety of Earthly life-forms and the vastness of the universe, it seemed improbable that only Earth provided conditions permissive of the origin and support of life. Gould staunchly opposed biological determinism, the assumption that biology determines individual differences, making them unchangeable. Believing that science could never be detached completely from a personal dimension because scientists are human, Gould often spoke about the cultural embeddedness of science, the fact that society influences scientific endeavors.

In 1981, the MacArthur Foundation awarded Gould a fellowship, nicknamed the "genius grant," awarded to U.S. residents or citizens who show exceptional merit and promise for continued and enhanced creative work. *Discover* magazine named Gould Scientist of the Year for 1981 for developing the theory of punctuated equilibrium. In 2000 the U.S. Library of Congress named him one of 83 living legends who have "advanced and embodied the quintessentially American ideal of individual creativity, conviction, dedication and exuberance." Gould also received the Medal of Excellence from Columbia University in 1983, the Silver Medal from the Zoological Society of London in 1984, the Gold Medal for Service to Zoology from the Linnean Society of London in 1992, and the Distinguished Scientist Award from the Center for the Study of Evolution and the Origin of Life at the University of California, Los Angeles in 1997. He helped found *Paleobiology*, a journal that publishes articles focusing on processes and patterns in biological paleontology. He also received over 40 honorary degrees and belonged to numerous scientific organizations including the National Academy of Sciences, the Paleontological Society, American Society of Naturalists, and the American Association for the Advancement of Science, for which he served as president in 2000. In 1996, Gould became the Vincent Astor Visiting Research Professor of Biology at New York University and divided his time between New York and Cambridge.

In 1982, Gould was diagnosed with mesothelioma, a type of abdominal cancer. Though the median survival time was eight months, he lived two more decades and died from an unrelated lung cancer on May 20, 2002. His is survived by his second wife, Rhonda Roland Shearer, and his two sons, Jesse and Ethan, from his first marriage.

Gould was fluent in several languages and could read sources in their original languages. He was also a New York Yankees fanatic and a gifted baritone who sang with the Boston Cecilia Society. Though the public recognized him as a famous paleontologist, he described himself as a historian at heart and never limited his studies to a particular field. Wherever answers could be found, Gould ventured there to find them. His intellect surpassed the ordinary, and associates described him as both brilliant and arrogant. Gould's research and writings on punctuated equilibrium strongly influenced ideas about macroevolution and loosened the restrictions of classical evolutionary theory. He demonstrated that stasis is an important phenomenon worthy of examination and that punctuation was an interesting model of change. Alongside discussions on Darwin and his contributions to modern evolutionary theory, modern textbooks of Earth science, paleontology, biology, and evolution all include descriptions of punctuated equilibrium. Only time will reveal how Gould's more recent ideas concerning the restructuring of evolutionary theory will influence future lessons on the history of life, but impressions of his philosophies will certainly be evident.

CHRONOLOGY

1941	Stephen Jay Gould is born on September 10 in New York City.
1963	Earns a bachelor's degree in geology and philosophy from Antioch College
1966	Becomes assistant professor of geology at Antioch College
1967	Receives a Ph.D. in paleontology from Columbia University and joins faculty at Harvard University as an assistant professor of geology and assistant curator of invertebrate paleontology

1971	Becomes associate professor of geology and associate curator of invertebrate paleontology at Harvard University
1972	Publishes paper, "Punctuated Equilibria: An Alternative to Phyletic Gradualism" with Niles Eldredge in *Models in Paleobiology*
1973	Is promoted to full professor of geology and curator of invertebrate paleontology at Harvard University
1974–2001	Writes 300 consecutive monthly essays for the column "This View of Life" in *Natural History* magazine
1975	The Paleontological Society awards Gould the Schuchert Award for excellence in paleontological research by a scientist less than 40 years of age
1981	Receives a genius grant from the MacArthur Foundation, is named Scientist of the Year by *Discover* magazine, and publishes *The Mismeasure of a Man*. Gould also serves as an expert witness in a lawsuit that challenged the constitutionality of an Arkansas law requiring biology teachers to teach intelligent design along with evolution
1982	Is named the Alexander Agassiz Professor of Zoology at Harvard University
1987	Publishes the book *Time's Arrow, Time's Cycle*
1989	Publishes the book *Wonderful Life: The Burgess Shale and the Nature of History*
1996	Becomes the Vincent Astor Visiting Research Professor of Biology at New York University
2002	Dies from lung cancer on May 20 in Manhattan, shortly after publishing *The Structure of Evolutionary Theory*

FURTHER READING

Encyclopedia of World Biography. Vol. 6, 2nd ed. Farmington Hills, Mich.: Thomson Gale, 1998. Brief biographies of notable figures and summaries of their accomplishments. Written for high school students.

Evory, Ann, and Linda Metzger, eds. *Contemporary Authors: New Revision Series.* Vol. 10. Farmington Hills, Mich.: Thomson Gale, 1983. Contains a limited but useful sketch on Gould's career and honors with a few sidelights.

Gould, Stephen Jay. *The Structure of Evolutionary Theory.* Cambridge, Mass.: Belknap Press, 2002. Gould's magnum opus, describing the integration of classical evolutionary theory and modern critiques, including a useful comprehensive bibliography of evolution literature. Difficult reading.

Olson, Richard, ed. *Biographical Encyclopedia of Scientists.* Vol. 2. New York: Marshall Cavendish, 1998. Clear, concise summary of major events in the scientists' lives at an accessible level.

The Unofficial Stephen Jay Gould Archive. Available online. URL: http://www.stephenjaygould.org. Accessed January 15, 2005. Put together by a college student, this site contains links to biographical profiles and interviews with Gould and other scientists, quotations, a bibliography of Gould's books and selected papers, and more.

GLOSSARY

allopatric speciation a mode of speciation that occurs when the ancestral population becomes separated by a geographical barrier

anatomy the scientific study of the structure of organisms

argillaceous a sedimentary rock formed from clay deposits

astronomy the study of the universe

basalt a dense, fine-grained igneous rock; the most common type of solidified lava

bedrock a fixed rock formation that may be exposed to view or covered by soil, vegetation, or sediments

brachiopod a marine invertebrate that has two valves that are not close copies of one another

catastrophism the belief that biological and geological phenomena are caused by catastrophes rather than uniform, continuous processes

catastrophist one who believes in catastrophism

chalk a soft, porous, fine-grained limestone, usually white in color, made mostly from very small fossil sea shells

clade a group of organisms sharing a common ancestor

coal a combustible organic sedimentary rock formed from compressed, decomposed plant remains

compound a substance made up of two or more elements

continent any of the seven great landmasses on the globe

continental drift a hypothesis suggesting that all present continents once existed as a single supercontinent and that they have been slowly moving around the surface of the globe since breaking apart 200 million years ago

convergent boundary places where the lithosphere is destroyed by recycling back into the mantle; where the edge of a tectonic plate sinks under its neighboring plate in a process called subduction

crust the outermost solid layer of the Earth, rests atop the mantle

delta a triangular deposit of sand and other sediments that collects at the mouths of some rivers

dip the angle in degrees between the horizontal and any inclined geological feature

divergent boundary the places where tectonic plates move apart from one another and new lithosphere is created

Earth science the study of the physical components of Earth (land, water, and air) and the processes that influence them

element a substance made up of only one type of atom

entomology the study of insects

erosion the gradual process of wearing away

evolution change over time

extant still in existence

extinct no longer existing

fault a fracture in the Earth's crust with the mass on one side being pushed up, down, or sideways

flint a hard granular quartz, usually found in chalk

fossil a remnant of an organism from a past geologic age usually found embedded in the Earth's crust

fossil succession the principle stating that fossil organisms succeed one another in a definite and determinable order; allows any time period to be recognized by its fossil content

geochronology the science of determining the time or length of existence for geological formations and periods

geological map a map that shows an area's BEDROCK formations or other geologic features, such as sediment deposits or glacial features

geology the scientific study of the origin, history, and structure of the Earth

geoscience a branch of Earth science dealing with the solid part of Earth, such as geology

glossopetrae fossilized shark teeth, once thought to be serpent tongues that magically were turned to stone and contained supernatural powers

Gondwanaland former southern supercontinent that contained what is now South America, Africa, India, Australia, and Antarctica

half-life a measure of the instability of a radioisotope; the amount of time required for one-half of a quantity of radioactive material to disintegrate

historical geologist a geologist that studies the Earth's history

ichthyology the study of fish

igneous one of three primary rock types found in Earth's crust, formed by the solidification of molten magma generated deep within the planet

intelligent design the nonscientific belief that a higher being created the Earth and its inhabitants

invertebrate lacking a backbone

isobar a line drawn on a weather map that connects places having the same average barometric pressure

isotherm a line drawn on a weather map that connects places having the same average temperature

isotope one of two or more atoms that have the same number of protons but a different number of neutrons in the nucleus, and therefore, have different atomic masses

lateral extension principle stating that a rock unit continues laterally unless there is a structure or change to prevent its extension

Laurasia a former northern supercontinent that contained what is now North America, Europe, and Asia

limestone a sedimentary rock made primarily of calcium carbonate, formed by the accumulation of remains of sea creatures or by chemical precipitation

lithology a description of the major macroscopic features of a type of rock, particularly texture, composition, and color; also the branch of geology devoted to the study of rock types

lymph a transparent, yellowish fluid that plays an important role in the immune system and in the transportation of certain materials throughout the body

magma   a body of molten rock found in the Earth's crust, including any dissolved gases and crystals; may be extruded by volcanic eruptions to form solid rock

mantle   the zone in the Earth between the hard crust and the liquid metallic core

marlstone   a half-formed ARGILLACEOUS limestone, containing a large proportion of clay, calcium carbonate, microfossils, and relic ooze

metallurgy   the science and technology of extracting metals from their ores, purifying metals, and creating useful items from metals

metamorphic rock   one of three basic rock types formed by the alteration of sedimentary or igneous rock by pressure, temperature, moisture, and time

meteorology   the study of the atmosphere

mid-oceanic ridge   an immense underwater mountain range more than 31,000 miles (50,000 km) long and 500 miles (800 km) wide

mineral   a naturally occurring, nonliving, homogenous solid with a definite chemical composition and a highly ordered atomic structure

mineralogy   the branch of geology devoted to the study of minerals

mining   the process of extracting minerals from the earth

natural selection   the process in nature by which organisms best adapted to their environment have better reproductive success than others

neptunism   a theory popularized by Werner stating that all rocks were precipitates from a primordial ocean

neptunist   one who believes in NEPTUNISM

oceanography   the scientific study of the oceans

oolite   a common limestone composed primarily of tiny spherical accretions of calcium carbonate around a quartz core

ore   a mineral or aggregate of minerals that is mined to obtain a substance it contains

original horizontality   law stating that sediments settling out from bodies of water are deposited horizontally in layers parallel to the Earth's surface

orogeny   the formation of mountains, especially by folding of the Earth's crust

osteological   relating to the anatomical study of bones

outcrop   the part of a rock unit that is exposed at the Earth's surface

paleobiology   the subdiscipline of paleontology that focuses on floral and faunal fossil species

paleoclimatology   the study of ancient climates

paleomagnetic   having to do with the direction of the residual magnetism in ancient rocks

paleontology   the systematic study of prehistoric plants and animals and of the history of life on Earth based on fossils

Pangaea   the supercontinent proposed to exist 200 million years ago that broke apart to form the present landmasses

pantograph   an instrument for mechanically copying a figure to any desired scale. It consists of a framework of slender, jointed metal rods that simultaneously reproduce a line or circle drawn by the operator

petrologist   one who studies the origin and composition of rocks

phyletic gradualism   a hypothesis stating that evolution occurs at a constant rate and that new species arise by the gradual transformation of ancestral species

physical geologist   a geologist who examines the materials of the Earth and seeks to understand the processes and forces that shape the Earth

plate tectonics   the theory proposing that the Earth's outer shell consists of individual plates that interact in various ways, producing earthquakes, volcanoes, mountains, and the crust itself

plutonist   one who believes the theory, advanced by Hutton, stating that almost all rocks originated as a result of heat and melting, rose from the mantle to form new land, only to decay and be regenerated; vulcanism

punctuated equilibrium   theory stating that evolution proceeds rapidly during speciation, then is followed by longer periods with no change; an explanation for the lack of transitional forms in the fossil record

radioactivity   the phenomenon of nuclear disintegration of unstable atoms, resulting in the emission of radiant energy

rock   a consolidated or unconsolidated aggregation of mineral or organic matter. Three primary types include sedimentary, igneous, and METAMORPHIC ROCK

sandstone   a sedimentary rock composed of sand-sized particles of silicates bound together by a cement such as clay or quartz

sediment   unconsolidated particles created from the weathering and erosion of rock, by chemical precipitations from solutions in water or from the secretions of organisms, and transported by water, wind, or glaciers

sedimentary rock   rock formed from the weathered products of preexisting rocks that have been transported, deposited, and lithified

shale   a type of sedimentary rock formed by the accumulation of clay particles; easily splits into thin layers

siliceous   containing the common mineral silica

siltstone   a fine-grained sandstone of consolidated silt

smelter   an establishment for melting ores to separate the metallic constituents

speciation   the creation of a new species by evolution

species   a particular kind of organism. Members possess similar anatomies and are able to interbreed, producing fertile offspring

stratification   the layered or bedded arrangement of rocks

stratigraphy   the study of layers of rock, their fossils, and the time periods during which they were laid down

stratum (plural **strata**)   a layer of sedimentary rock, usually within a column of overlaid parallel layers

strike   the direction taken by a structural surface as it intersects the horizontal. Strike is 90 degrees to the direction of dip

subduction   the process where one tectonic plate is forced underneath another at a convergent boundary

superposition   law of stratigraphy stating that within an undisturbed column of rock, the oldest strata occur on the bottom and the younger beds are on the top

survey to measure for size and boundaries using linear and angular measurements and applying geometry and trigonometry so as to construct a map or detailed description

Terebratulid order of small brachiopods

Tertiary one of the great and more recent divisions of the geological timescale; the period of the Cenozoic Era that includes the Paleocene, Eocene, Oligocene, Miocene, and Pliocene Epochs

theodolite a surveying instrument for measuring angles and directions

transform plate boundary a boundary or fault where tectonic plates slide horizontally alongside one another; often the site of earthquakes

unconformity a surface that represents a break in the rock record; caused by erosion or nondeposition

uniformitarianism principle stating that processes that shaped the Earth in the geologic past are essentially the same as those operating today

uranium a radioactive, metallic chemical element with the atomic number 92

Variscan a major orogeny, occurring during the Carboniferous and Permian Periods, relating to the closure of the gap between Africa and Europe. It resulted in the building of many central European mountain chains

vein a deposit of mineral, usually crystalline, limited to a fissure or joint of a rock

vertebrate a chordate animal that has a backbone, includes the classes mammals, birds, fish, reptiles, and amphibians

vulcanism (also **volcanism**) volcanic force or activity; also the theory advanced by Hutton, stating that almost all rocks originated as a result of heat and melting, rose from the mantle to form new land, only to decay and be regenerated

vulcanist one who believes in vulcanism

weathering process where the action of air and water slowly cause rocks to break apart and disintegrate, forming debris in the form of gravel, sand, and silt

FURTHER RESOURCES

Books

Dasch, E. Julius, ed. *Earth Sciences for Students*. 4 vols. New York: Macmillan Reference USA, 1999. Comprehensive coverage that contains definitions in margins and numerous illustrations, written for young adults.

———. *Macmillan Encyclopedia of Earth Sciences*. 2 vols. New York: Macmillan Reference USA, 1996. Complete overview of the Earth sciences, written for high school students.

The Diagram Group. *The Facts On File Earth Science Handbook*. New York: Facts On File, 2000. Convenient resource containing a glossary of terms, short biographical profiles of celebrated Earth scientists, a chronology of events and discoveries, and useful charts, tables, and diagrams.

Duff, Peter McLaren Donald, ed. *Holmes' Principles of Physical Geology*. 4th ed. London: Chapman and Hall, 1993. A recent edition of Holmes's classic textbook edited by a former student and colleague.

Erickson, Jon. *Historical Geology: Understanding Our Planet's Past*. New York: Facts On File, 2002. Chronicles the formation and evolution of Earth to explain the current geological conditions.

———. *Making of the Earth: Geologic Forces that Shape Our Planet*. New York: Facts On File, 2000. Describes how the surface of the Earth constantly changes by processes such as erosion and uplifting, plate tectonics, and catastrophic collapse.

Faul, Henry, and Carol Faul. *It Began With a Stone: A History of Geology from the Stone Age to the Age of Plate Tectonics*. New York:

John Wiley, 1983. Describes the development of the Earth sciences from antiquity to modern time.

Gates, Alexander E. *A to Z of Earth Scientists.* New York: Facts On File, 2002. Profiles more than 150 Earth scientists, discussing their research and contributions. Includes bibliography, cross-references, and chronology.

Geikie, Archibald. *Founders of Geology.* New York: Macmillan and Company, 1897. Old but classic text on the first geologists written by an expert in the field.

Mathez, Edmond A. *Earth: Inside and Out.* New York: The New Press, 2001. Summary of the Earth, its origin, evolution, and processes, written for general readers.

Moody, R., A. Zhuravlev, D. Dixon, and I. Jenkins. *Atlas of the Evolving Earth.* 3 vols. New York: Macmillan Reference USA, 2001. Overview of the Earth's complex development organized by geological period.

Oldroyd, David. *Thinking about the Earth: A History of Ideas in Geology.* Cambridge, Mass.: Harvard University Press, 1996. Comprehensive survey of the early ideas in geology but difficult to read.

Pentland, Peter, and Pennie Stoyles. *Earth Science.* Philadelphia, Pa.: Chelsea House, 2003. Simplified answers to complicated questions about Earth science, written for juvenile readers.

Wiggers, Raymond. *The Amateur Geologist: Explorations and Investigations.* New York: Franklin Watts, 1993. Gives a basic overview of geology for young adults, sends the reader on three geological investigations from home, and contains science fair project ideas and a glossary.

Woodhead, James A., ed. *Earth Science.* 5 vols. Pasadena, Calif.: Salem Press, 2001. Contains approximately 500 lengthy introductory essays on selected topics in Earth science.

Internet Resources

Bob's Rock Shop. Available online. URL: http://www.rockhounds.com. Accessed November 3, 2004. Contains many images of rocks and minerals as well as links for news articles about rocks, rock and mineral identification keys, and more of interest for rock and mineral enthusiasts.

Cascades Volcano Observatory. U.S. Department of the Interior, U.S. Geological Survey. Available online. URL: http://vulcan. wr.usgs.gov. Last updated December 16, 2004. Contains information about volcanoes and other natural hazards such as earthquakes and landslides.

Destination Earth. National Aeronautics and Space Administration. Available online. URL: http://earth.nasa.gov/flash_top.html. Last updated June 22, 2004. All about the Earth sciences, history, present, and future. Contains links for learning games, research opportunities, and physical, geophysical, and biochemical databases.

Directorate for Geosciences. National Science Foundation. Available online. URL: http://www.geo.nsf.gov. Last modified April 22, 2004. Divided into "Atmospheric," "Earth," and "Ocean" sciences. Explore each to site to learn about the division, an explanation of the field, links for further resources, funding opportunities, and more.

Discover the History of Life. University of California–Berkeley Museum of Paleontology. Available online. URL: http://www. ucmp.berkeley.edu/historyoflife/histoflife.html. Accessed January 15, 2005. Contains links to online exhibits on phylogeny, geologic time, and evolution, as well as educational programs for all levels.

Earth Floor. Wheeling Jesuit University/NASA Classroom of the Future. Available online. URL: http://www.cotf.edu/ete/modules/ msese/earthsys.html. Accessed February 21, 2005. Supported by a NASA Information Infrastructure Technology Application Program, this online educational resource teaches students about the Earth and its processes through modules and problem-based activities.

Earth Observatory. National Aeronautics and Space Administration. Available online. URL: http://earthobservatory.nasa.gov. Accessed January 15, 2005. Public site for scientific information and satellite imagery of planet Earth, focuses on the Earth's climate and environmental change.

Earth Science World. American Geological Institute. Available online. URL: http://www.earthscienceworld.org. Accessed January 15, 2005. Contains an image bank, an interactive geological timescale, information on careers in geosciences, an interactive game about oil exploration, and climate data from around the world.

Geochemistry of Igneous Rocks. Geokem. Available online. URL: http://geokem.com. Last updated January 15, 2005. An e-text of geochemical data interpretation. Contains general information about the geochemistry and petrology fields but is a bit advanced for secondary students.

Hall of Planet Earth. American Museum of Natural History. Available online. URL: http://www.amnh.org/rose/hope. Accessed January 15, 2005. Based on the Gottesman Hall of Planet Earth, this site includes links to exhibition highlights on a variety of subjects, including the Earth's conception, its geological formations, and how scientists gather information about Earth's history from the rocks. Follow the link to the AMNH Earth Bulletin for information on new developments in Earth science.

Rockdoctor. Available online. URL: http://www.cobweb.net/~bug2/rock1.htm. Accessed January 15, 2005. Provides basic information for identifying common minerals and rocks as well as some basic information about the Earth's interior and seismology.

USGS Home Page. U.S. Department of the Interior, U.S. Geological Survey. Available online. URL: http://www.usgs.gov. Last modified September 13, 2004. Federal source for reliable science about the Earth, its natural and living resources, natural hazards, and the environment. Follow link titled "Our Science" for specific subject information.

Volcano World. Department of Space Studies, University of North Dakota. Available online. URL: http://volcano.und.nodak.edu. Accessed January 15, 2004. This easy-to-navigate site is full of information relating to volcanoes. Explore the "Teaching and Learning" link to find volcanic facts, additional resources, and information on becoming a volcanologist.

Windows to the Universe. *Our Planet.* Boulder, Colo.: ©2000–04 University Corporation of Atmospheric Research (UCAR), ©1995–1999, 2000. The Regents of the University of Michigan. Available online. URL: http://www.windows.ucar. edu. Accessed January 15, 2005. Makes learning about topics such as the Earth's interior and surface, magnetosphere, and geology fun.

Periodicals

American Scientist

Published by Sigma Xi, The Scientific Research Society
P.O. Box 13975
3106 East NC Highway 54
Research Triangle Park, NC 27709
Telephone: (919) 549-0097 or (800) 282-0444
www.amsci.org
Bimonthly magazine containing articles on science and technology

Discover

Published by Buena Vista Magazines
114 Fifth Avenue
New York, NY 10011
Telephone: (212) 633-4400
www.discover.com
A popular monthly magazine containing easy to understand articles on a variety of scientific topics

Geology

Published by The Geological Society of America
P.O. Box 9140
Boulder, CO 80301-9140
Telephone: (303) 447-2020
www.geosociety.org/pubs
Widely read monthly Earth science journal

GSA Bulletin

Published by The Geological Society of America
P.O. Box 9140
Boulder, CO 80301-9140
Telephone: (303) 447-2020
www.geosociety.org/pubs
Publishes classic style research papers in all the Earth science disciplines

GSA Today

Published by The Geological Society of America
P.O. Box 9140
Boulder, CO 80301-9140
Telephone: (303) 447-2020
www.geosociety.org/pubs
Contains features and news about Earth science

Nature

The Macmillan Building
4 Crinan Street
London N1 9XW
United Kingdom
Telephone: +44 (0)20 7833 4000
www.nature.com/nature
A prestigious primary source of scientific literature

Science

Published by the American Association for the Advancement of
  Science
1200 New York Avenue NW
Washington, DC 20005
Telephone: (202) 326-6417
www.sciencemag.org
One of the most highly regarded primary sources of scientific research

Scientific American
415 Madison Avenue
New York, NY 10017
Telephone: (212) 754-0550
www.sciam.com
A popular monthly magazine that publishes articles on a broad range of subjects and current issues in science and technology

Societies and Organizations

American Association for the Advancement of Science (www.aaas.org) 1200 New York Avenue NW, Washington, DC 20005. Telephone: (202) 326-6400

American Geophysical Union (www.agu.org) 2000 Florida Avenue NW, Washington, DC 20009-1277. Telephone: (202) 462-6900 or (800) 966-2481

The Geological Society of America (www.geosociety.org) P.O. Box 9140, Boulder, CO 80301-9140. Telephone: (303) 447-2020

The Geological Society of London (www.geolsoc.org.uk) Burlington House, Piccadilly, London W1J 0BG, United Kingdom. Telephone: +44 (0)20 7434 9944

The Mineralogical Society (www.minersoc.org) 41 Queen's Gate, London SW75HR, United Kingdom. Telephone: +44 (0)20 7584 7516

Index

Italic page numbers indicate illustrations.

A

Abstract of a Dissertation . . . Concerning the System of the Earth, Its Duration, and Stability (Hutton) 38
Age of the Earth, The (Holmes) 124, 127
A Geological Section from London to Snowdon (Smith) 89
Agricola, Georgius *1*, 1–10, xx
  birth of 2
  chronology of 9–10
  death of 9
  education of 2
  marriage of 2, 3
air pressure *54*
allopatric speciation 141
ammonium chloride 33
analogous structures 72
Anatomical Observations on Glands (Steno) 16
anatomy 15, 64–65
angle constancy, law of 26
angular unconformity formation *36*
Animal Kingdom, Distributed According to Its Organization, The (Cuvier) 71
Anning, Mary 84–85
Apollo 11 xiii
Aristotle 18
Armstrong, Neil xiii
Art of Measuring, The (Fenning) 78
Aston, William Francis 127–128
astronomy xx
Atlantic Ocean, coasts in *107*

B

Bailey, Edward 103
Bakewell, Robert 94
Balfour, Sarah 32
Banks, Joseph 86
Bartholin, Thomas 15

basalt 54
Bauer, Gregor 2
Becquerel, Henri 119
Bermannus; sive de re metallica dialogues (Bermannus; or a dialogue on metallurgy [Agricola]) 3, 6
Bible 15, 21, 34, xix. *See also* Genesis
biology, definition of 43
Black, Joseph 33, 34
Black Death 6, 14
Bläes, Gerhard 16
Boltwood, Bertram 121
Bonpland, Aimé 45
Borch, Ole 14, 18
boundaries, in plate tectonics 112
Brongniart, Alexandre 67–68, 83
Brown, Harrison 131
Buch, Leopold von 95
Buckland, William 94, 96–97

C

carbon dating 122–123
carbon dioxide 33, 48
Cartesian philosophy 18–19
Cary, John 87
catastrophism 38, 70, 97, xix
Catholicism 22, 24
Central Asia (von Humboldt) 58
chalk 32–33, *69*
Charles IV (king of Spain) 45
Charles Lyell (Bailey) 103
clay, plastic *69*
coastlines 107, *107*
continental drift 49, 105–106, 107–114, *109*, *113*
convergent boundaries 112
Cook, James 44
Copley Medal
  Alexander von Humboldt receives 58
  Charles Lyell receives 103
Cosmos (von Humboldt) 58

crust, of Earth 25, 37, 112–114, *113*, 118
crystal formation 26, 38
Curie, Marie 119
Curie, Pierre 119
Cuvier, Georges *61*, 61–74, 83, xx
  birth of 62
  chronology of 73–74
  death of 72
  education of 62
  marriage of 65
  meets Charles Lyell 95
  as professor 63

D

Darwin, Charles 58, 102, 138, 140–141
dating, radiometric 118–125
decomposition 65
deism 34
Delineation of the Strata of England and Wales, with Part of Scotland, A (Smith) 87
De natura fossilum (On the nature of fossils; Agricola) 2, 5
De ortu et causis subterraneorum (On the emergence of materials from underground [Agricola] 4
De peste (On the plague; Agricola) 6
deposition *36*
De prima ac simplici institutione grammatica (On the elements and simple instruction of grammar [Agricola]) 2
De re metallica (On metallurgy [Agricola]) 4
Descartes, René 17, 18–20
De solido intra solidum naturaliter contento dissertaionis prodromus (Forerunner to a dissertation on solids naturally enclosed in solids [Steno]) 24–25, 27
diamonds 56

Dickinson, Emily 118
Die Enstenhung der Kontinente und Ozeane (The Origin of Continents and Oceans [Wegener]) 108, 126
Dietz, Robert Sinclair 111
dinosaurs 85, 96
dip (property of strata) 83
Discourse on the Anatomy of the Brain (Steno) 17–18
Discourse on the Method of Rightly Conducting One's Reason (Descartes) 18
Discourse on the Revolution of the Surface of the Globe (Cuvier) 70–71
dissection 17, 18
Distinguished Scientist Award, awarded to Stephen Jay Gould 147
divergent boundaries 112

E

Earth
  age of 23, 34, 118, 119, 123
  continuous formation of 35–38
  crust of 25, 37, 112–114, *113*, 118
  magnetic field of 57
  mantle of 57
  poles of 57
earth science
  definition of xx
eels, electric 47
Ehrenberg, Christian Gottfried 55
Eldredge, Niles 138, 139
Elements of Geology (Lyell) 100
Elements of Muscular Knowledge (Steno) 21
elephants 64–65
engineering, mining 2
Enlightenment, Age of xix
entomology 94
epistemology 19
epochs 100
Erasmus, Desiderius 2, 3
erosion 33, 34, *36*, xix
evolution 140–141, 144–146
extinction 61–62, 67–71, 99

F

fault lines 112
Fenning, Daniel 78
Ferdinando II de' Medici (grand duke of Tuscany) 20
flint 32, *69*
folding *36*

Forster, Georg 44
fossil(s)
  Agricola's work with 5–6
  beds, differences in 68
  formation of 22
  identifying animals from 64–67
  image of large quadruped 66
  Steno's work with 15–16, 22–23
  types of 64–65
fossil fuels 64
fossil succession 83

G

Galen 2
Gay-Lussac, Joseph 54
gazelles 67
generation, spontaneous 20
Geoffroy Saint-Hilaire, Étienne 71–72
geography, planet 53
geological chronology 25, 68, 117–118
Geological Description of the Paris Region (Cuvier & Brongniart) 68
Geological Evidences of the Antiquity of Man, The (Lyell) 102
geological mapping 87–89, *88*
geological time scale *80*, 100, 131, *131*
geologic cycle 37
geomagnetism 57
glaciers 37
Glen Roy *98*
glossopetrae 21–22
Gold Medal for Service, awarded to Stephen Jay Gould 147
Gould, Eleanor Rosenberg 138
Gould, Ethan 148
Gould, Jesse 148
Gould, Leonard 138
Gould, Stephen Jay *137*, 137–149, xx
  awards of 147
  birth of 138
  chronology of 148–149
  education of 138–139
  marriage of 139
gradual speciation 141
granite 38
Greece, ancient xix
Greenough, George Bellas 87, 89, 90
Gryphaea 142

guano 52
gypsum *69*

H

half-life 128–131
Hall, James 40–41
heart 18–19, 27–28
Hen's Teeth and Horse's Toes (Gould) 143
Hess, Harry Hammond 111, xx
Hippocrates 2
historical geologists xx
Hollwege, Maria Elizabeth von 44
Holmes, Arthur *117*, 117–134, xx
  awards of 132
  birth of 118
  chronology of 133–134
  death of 133
  education of 118, 120
  marriage of 124
Holmes, David 118
Holmes, Geoffrey 125
Holmes, Norman 125
homologous structures 72
horizontality, original 14, 25–26
Horner, Mary Elizabeth 100
Howe, Margaret 124
Humboldt, Alexander Georg von 44
Humboldt, Alexander von *43*, 43–60, xx
  birth of 44
  chronology of 59–60
  death of 58
  education of 44–45
  meets Charles Lyell 95
  receives Copley Medal 58
"Hume and Uniformitarianism" (Gould) 139
Hutton, James *31*, 31–42, xx
  birth of 32
  chronology of 40–42
  education of 32
  Charles Lyell and 94, 99
  opposition to 38–39
Hutton, William 32

I

ibis 71
igneous matter 35
I Have Landed (Gould) 143
Illustrations of the Huttonian Theory (Playfair) 39
immune system 15
intelligent design 144

Introduction to Geology
(Bakewell) 94
isobars 54, *54*
isotherms 54, *54*

J

Jefferson, Thomas 53
John Paul II (pope) 27
Johnstone, Sir John Vanden
Bempde 90
Joly, John 118, 119
Jones, Lady Elizabeth 79, 82

K

Kelvin, William Thompson,
Lord 118, 119, 120
Kirwan, Richard 38
Koch, J. P. 108
Köppen, Else 108

L

Laborde, Albert 119–120
Lamarck, Jean-Baptiste de
Monet de 71
lapidifying juice 5, 22
lateral continuity 14
lateral extension 26
law of angle constancy 26
Lawson, Bob 124–125
lead 128–131
Leclerc, Georges-Louis 62
Lee, Deborah 139
Libby, Willard Frank 123
limestone 38, *69*
logic 18–19
Lutheranism 22
Lyell, Charles *93*, 93–104, xx
birth of 94
chronology of 103–104
education of 94–95
James Hutton and 94, 99
knighting of 102
marriage of 100
Lyell, Charles, Sr. 94
Lyell Medal 103
lymph nodes 6, 15

M

maggots 20
magma 35, 48
magnetism 57. *See also*
paleomagnetism
mapping, geological 87–89, *88*
marlstone 79
mass spectrography 127–128
Maurice, Duke 4
Meaning of Evolution, The
(Simpson) 138
Medal of Excellence, awarded
to Stephen Jay Gould 147

Medici, Ferdinando de'. See
Ferdinando II de' Medici
Medici, Leopoldo de' 20
Meditations on First Philosophy
(Descartes) 18, 19
Megalosaurus 96
Meiner, Anna 2
*Memoir on the Species of
Elephants, Both Living and
Fossils* (Cuvier) 64
metallurgy 2, 3, 4–5, 6, 9
meteorology xx
*Mineral Geography of the Paris
Region* (Cuvier &
Brongniart) 68
mineralogy 1–2
minerals 1, 4, 5, 6
mining 3, 4–5, 6, *8*, 9, 45,
79–82
mining engineering 2
mining equipment 7
Mismeasure of Man, The
(Gould) 143–144
mountain building 37
mountain climbing 50–52
mummification 71
Murchison, Roderick 96
Murchison Medal, awarded to
Arthur Holmes 132
muscular contraction 20–22
Musée National d'Histoire
Naturelle (National Museum
of Natural History) 63

N

Napoleon 53
Napoleonic Wars 45
Natural History (Leclerc) 62
natural selection 73
neptunists 34, 38, 40–41
Nielsdatter, Anne 14
Nier, Alfred 128, 130–131
nitrogen 48
Nobel Prize, awarded to
Willard Libby 123

O

oceanography xx
On Man (Descartes) 19
On Muscles and Glands (Steno)
16
On the Origin of Species
(Darwin) 102, 140
opossums 67
ores 5, 9
original horizontality 14, 25–26
otters 67
outcrops 52
ovaries 24
oyster bed *69*
Oyster Club 33

P

paleobiology 137–138
paleoclimatology 110
paleomagnetism 111. *See also*
magnetism
paleontological stratigraphy
68, *69*
paleontology 2, 65
Panda's Thumb, The (Gould)
143
Pangaea 79, 108–110, *109*,
112, 114
parotid glands 16
Patterson, Clair 131
Pedersen, Sten 14
Penrose Medal, awarded to
Arthur Holmes 132
petrification 64–65. *See also*
fossils
petrology 118
Pfaff, Christian Heinrich 63
Phillips, John 86
philosophy 18–20
phosphates 52
phyletic gradualism 140, *142*
physical geologists xx
pineal gland 19, 20
Pius XI (pope) 27
plague 6, 14
planet geography 53
plate tectonics 112–114, *113*
Playfair, John 39
Plesiosaurus macrocephalus 85
plutonists 32
*Political Essay on the Island of
Cuba* (von Humboldt) 48–49
Prévost, Constant 95
Principles of Geology (Lyell) 93,
99, 102, xx
Principles of Physical Geology
(Holmes) 132
*Prodromus. See De solido intra
solidum naturaliter contento
dissertaionis prodromus*
(Forerunner to a dissertation
on solids naturally enclosed
in solids; Steno)
Pterosaur 85
"Punctuated Equilibria: An
Alternative to Phyletic
Gradualism" (Gould &
Eldridge) 140
punctuated equilibrium (PE)
138, *142*, 142–143
pundibs 78

R

radioactivity 119, 126–127. *See
also* carbon dating;
radiometric dating
Redi, Francesco 20

refining 9
Relics of the Deluge (Buckland) 97
Rennie, John 82
reproduction 24
Researches on Fossil Bones of Quadrupeds (Cuvier) 70
Reynolds, Doris L. 127
Richardson, Benjamin 85
Rose, Gustav 55
Royal Medal, awarded to Charles Lyell 103
Rutherford, Ernest 119

S

salivary duct 16–17
sandstone 69
Schuchert Award, awarded to Stephen Jay Gould 143
Schütz, Anna 3
scientific method xiii–xiv
Scientific Revolution xix
seafloor spreading 111
"seashell question" 15–16
Second Visit to the United States of North America, A (Lyell) 101
sediment 23. 37, 25
sedimentary rock 25
Seeking Truth in the Sciences (Descartes) 18
Seifert, Karl 55
shale 79
shark teeth 21–22
Shearer, Rhonda Roland 148
siliceous pebbles 97
Silver Medal, awarded to Stephen Jay Gould 147
Simpson, George Gaylord 138
smelters 5, 9
Smith, Ann 78
Smith, John 78
Smith, Mary Ann 86
Smith, William 77, 77–92, xx
  birth of 78
  chronology of 91–92
  death of 90
  marriage of 86
  medal in honor of 91
  receives Wollaston Medal 90
soil erosion 33
Somerset Canal 81, 82
Soto, Nicholás 47
spaceflight xiii
speciation 141
spontaneous generation 20

Squaloraja 85
Steno, Nicolaus 13, 13–28, xx
  birth of 14
  chronology of 28–29
  death of 27
  education of 14–15
  sainthood of 27
Stensen, Niels. *See* Steno, Nicolaus
strata 23, 25, 35, 69, 88, xix
  Cuvier's work on 68–70
  definition of 13
  Hutton's work on 35, 37–38
  Lyell's work on 96–99
Strata Identified by Organized Fossils (Smith) 89
Stratigraphical System of Organized Fossils Part I (Smith) 89
stratigraphy 68, 69
strike (property of strata) 83
Structure of Evolutionary Theory (Gould) 144
Strutt, Robert J. 120
subduction 112
subsidence 36
sulfur dioxide 48
supercontinent 79
superposition 13
surveying 6

T

terebratulids 78
"Theory of the Earth; or an Investigation of the Laws Observable in the Composition, Dissolution, and Restoration of Land Upon the Globe" (Hutton) 33–34
Theory of the Earth with Proofs and Illustrations (Hutton) 39
Thermodynamik der Atmosphäre (Thermodynamics of the atmosphere; Wegener) 106
Thirty Years' War 14
thorium 119
Time's Arrow, Time's Cycle (Gould 139
Townsend, Joseph 85
transform plate boundaries 112
Travels in North America (Lyell) 101
typhoid fever 46

U

unconformities 35–36, 36
uniformitarianism 93, 99, 139, xix
uplifting 36
uranium 119, 128–130

V

Variscan Orogeny 79
veins, mineral 5, 37–38
vestigial organs 72
Vetlesen Prize, awarded to Arthur Holmes 132
Viviani, Vincenzo 26
volcanoes 5, 26, 35, 48–49, xix
Voyages to the Equinoctial Regions of the New Continent Made During the Years 1799 to 1804 (von Humboldt) 54, 54
vulcanists 32, 97

W

Wallace, Alfred 58
water, in theory of Earth's formation 34, 37
Watts, William 120
weathering 34
Webb, Edward 78
Wegener, Alfred 49, 105, 105–116, xx
  birth of 106
  chronology of 115–116
  education of 106
  marriage of 108
Wegener, Anna Schwartz 106
Wegener, Richard 106
Werner, Abraham Gottlob 34, 38, 53–54, 94
William Smith Medal 91
Wollaston Medal
  awarded to William Buckland 97
  awarded to Arthur Holmes 132
  awarded to Charles Lyell 103
  awarded to William Smith 90
Wonderful Life: The Burgess Shale and the Nature of History (Gould) 144

Z

Zoological Philosophy (Lamarck) 71